Carnal Knowledge of God

Carnal Knowledge of God

Embodied Love and the Movement for Justice

Rebecca M. M. Voelkel

Fortress Press
Minneapolis

CARNAL KNOWLEDGE OF GOD

Embodied Love and the Movement for Justice

Cover design: Rob Dewey

Print ISBN: 978-1-5064-2045-5

eBook ISBN: 978-1-5064-2046-2

The paper used in this publication meets the minimum requirements of American National Standard for Information Sciences — Permanence of Paper for Printed Library Materials, ANSI Z329.48-1984.

Manufactured in the U.S.A.

This book was produced using Pressbooks.com, and PDF rendering was done by PrinceXML.

Dedicated to the Rev. Dr. Marilyn McCord Adams, my teacher, mentor, and friend whose love and passion helped give birth to this book. "Be outrageous for the gospel's sake and fiercely trust in the goodness of God in the face of evil."

Contents

Acknowledgments

Even as I acknowledge my responsibility for the shape, form, and content of this book, I am profoundly aware that it has been birthed out of an extended community whose body is big and bodacious and powerful. To the women and genderqueer people who took the time to share their wisdom and insights, some of them borne of pain and suffering, I return thanks to God for you.

To all those religious communities that have guided and shaped my development as a theologian and activist—the United Church of Christ (UCC), the Center for the Prevention of Sexual and Domestic Violence, the World Council of Churches US Urban-Rural Mission, St. Paul's UCC, St. John's UCC, St. Luke's UCC, the Peoples Church of Chicago, Earlham College Meeting for Worship, Pilgrim Congregational UCC, Spirit of the Lakes UCC, Lyndale UCC, the Christian Base Communities in Mexico and El Salvador, Earlham College, Yale Divinity School, and United Theological Seminary of the Twin Cities—I would not have been able to write word one without you. I hope you know who you are. In particular, I need to thank my colleague, Fintan Moore, whose shared dreaming about sex and the spirit helped me begin to systematize my thinking. *Míle buíochas libh!* (A Thousand Thanks!) Your queerly passionate, profanity-laden reverence remains a guiding gift.

I also stand on the shoulders of countless activists and saints whose walking made the path on which they and I have been able to tread. Abolitionist, Suffrage, anti-war, Civil Rights, Black Power, feminist, womanist, mujerista, liberation, queer, and countless other movements have given birth to people who believed that they were called to make the world better and more just by acting together in faith. My imagination is bigger and broader because of them.

One of the activist communities to which I owe gratitude is the National LGBTQ Task Force. While I worked there, many of my colleagues talked through much of what I share here. Thank you in particular to Lisa Weiner-Mahfuz, Russell Roybal, Sue Hyde, David Lohman, Barbara Satin, Evangeline Weiss, Trina Olson, Sayre Reece, Trystan Reese, Causten Rodriguez-Wollerman, Kathleen Campisano, Rev. Darlene Nipper, Jack Harrison-Quintana, and Dr. J'aime Grant. Thank you for your patience and grace. I also would never have come to this point in my journey without the brilliant minds and wise hearts of my colleagues on the Welcoming Church Program Leaders, the Bishops and Elders Council, and the National Religious Leadership Roundtable. My participation in the Welcoming Religious Movement has taught me how to be a better theologian and pastor. In particular, Beth Zemsky helped put language to much of my movement-building impulses and experiences. This book and my work are more intentional and better because of you.

As I have worked, prayed, and struggled with all that is represented here, Rev. Debra Peevey has journeyed with me as my spiritual director, mentor, and friend. Her constant advice to pause and breathe remains powerful, embodied wisdom. You cannot be in your body—and honoring it—unless you first breathe and bring yourself to it.

Many scholars and mentors supported me along the way: Rev. Dr. Jann Cather Weaver, Dr. Jean Morris Trumbauer, Rev. Dr. Carolyn Pressler, Rev. Dr. Anita Bradshaw, Rev. Carol Wise, Darla Baker, Rev. Cath Crooks, Dr. Caroline Higgins, Dr. Jean Chagnon, Macky Alston, and Dr. Sharon Groves provided much supportive and precise feedback. Lisa Anderson was a critical accountability and thought partner. And when I hit a wall and thought I could not possibly see this project to the end, Rev. Dr. Shannon Craigo-Snell and Rev. Dr. Marilyn McCord Adams told me they believed in my work. In particular, Marilyn invited me to her home for a retreat, during which she painstakingly read over every word and then read draft after draft, offering concrete and clear feedback. I owe more than I can ever repay. Each piece helped make this work better. More recently, I have been challenged and supported by my colleagues in MARCH (Multifaith Anti-Racism, Change and Healing), in Healing Minnesota Stories, in Black Clergy United for Change, in Black Lives Matter Minneapolis, and in Minnesota Interfaith Power and Light. For scholars and mentors like you, I thank God.

Particularly in the later stages of this project, Nokomis Beach Coffee became my "office" and walks around my beloved Lake Nokomis grounded me and reminded me of the beauty of God's creation and my connection to it. A deep word of gratitude for Dennis, Mary, Miriam, Nichole, Ewa, Olivia, Nick, Zoe, and Jess, who offered me iced tea, even in the depth of Minnesota winters, and words of encouragement to fortify the work.

As I have been in the final editing phases, I have been asked to #StandwithStandingRock and be physically present with the Water Protectors there. My experience has both confirmed what I share in these pages and challenged me to greater faithfulness in the face of colonization.

None of what is shared here would have seen much of the light of day without the insightful, supportive, creatively critical eye of Neil Elliott, my editor at Fortress Press. I also am so grateful for the whole Fortress Press team, including Layne Johnson, Allyce Amundson, Tanner Hall, Esther Diley, Katie Clifford, Michael Moore, and Carolyn Halvorson. For their willingness to receive this manuscript and shepherd its coming into published form, I will remain forever grateful.

Finally, I want to thank my family. My mom and dad, Rev. Marguerite Unwin Voelkel and Rev. Bill Voelkel, both United Church of Christ pastors, laid the groundwork that has led me on this path. My dad died as I was writing the first drafts, and his spirit—most palpably represented in the picture of him that sits on my desk—helped keep me on the task. My partner, Maggie Shannon George, and our daughter, Shannon MacKenzie George Voelkel, allowed me time and space to germinate, incubate, and hold in my body much of what ended up on these pages. They also brought me food, beautiful pictures, and hugs and kisses. I love you both!

One note as you begin reading: throughout this work, I use terms that are important in the movement for embodied justice but that may be less familiar to many of my readers. To aid in clarity and understanding, please refer to the glossary that is included at the end of the book.

Introduction: Called to Be Lovers in the Name of God

When I was a child visiting my Grandmother Voelkel, I was often sent off to sleep before the adults. I always stayed in the bedroom next to the living room, sleeping on a bed made up on the floor. As I lay there, I could hear the murmurs of the ongoing conversation. In order to help myself fall asleep, I would trace the pieces, patterns, and varying textures of the quilt that was my sleeping cover. To this day, there is an inexorable connection between the pieces of that quilt and the stories of family, meaning, and connection that murmured around me as I fell into sleep.

In many ways, the how and the why of this book are like that quilt. There are distinct pieces and parts, but they are tied to the stories of family, meaning, and connection. The first one starts with me as a young, white, Midwestern girl.

I was an avid fan of the TV series *Little House on the Prairie*, adapted from the famous novels that chronicled the life of a young woman, Laura Ingalls Wilder, played by Melissa Gilbert. In what ended up being an early, telltale sign of my sexual orientation, I had a huge crush on Laura. I watched faithfully every week to see my shero tackle yet another daunting task of life on the prairie. In 1983, Melissa Gilbert starred in a made-for-TV movie entitled *Choices of the Heart* that told the story of Jean Donovan, one of the four US churchwomen who were raped and murdered in El Salvador in 1980 by US-backed Salvadoran death squads. The film changed the course of my life.p

All the admiration and love I felt for Melissa Gilbert as Laura Ingalls Wilder, I transferred to Jean Donovan. I wanted to know as many details about her life as I could find. I wanted to understand what motivated her, what had shaped her faith, how she had allowed her heart and life to be changed. I got that feeling that is somewhere between giddiness and insatiable curiosity about this person whose life seemed to be speaking directly to me. I read every book I could find on her, including biographies, books on Archbishop Óscar Romero (whose assassination nine months before Jean's had greatly impacted her ministry), and liberation theology from the Latin American context.

Jean's life story, and the subsequent consciousness I gained from the passion I felt for her, led me to sign the Pledge of Resistance, a document whose signatories promised to resist if the United States ever invaded El Salvador. It led me to start a chapter of Amnesty International at my high school, help host a conference on children of war, and participate in the Sanctuary Movement. And, in 1987, as a first-year student in college, it led me to participate in an "accompaniment" trip to El Salvador.

This early experience made me start to ask questions about the possible overlaps, connections, and synchronicities between sexuality, religious practice, and justice work. In retrospect, I smile at the thought that something as seemingly shallow as a crush on a TV star became that place and occasion for God's desire to be revealed to me. I also smile at the way in which God's humor, imagination, and depth of purpose are all interwoven with my early desire. What I learned was that my own passions, which were markers of both my sexuality and my faith, led me toward one particular person but also drew me into her passions and the communities and justice work for which she labored. And my own religious fervor was informed and changed because of the religious fervor of both that person and the community with whom she ministered.

The second quilt piece that informs the how and why of this book came a few years later. I was a first-year student in seminary when my other grandmother, Grammie, died. She was a Scottish immigrant who had graduated first in her class from sixth grade but had to enter the work force at age twelve to support her family. I was her only grandchild and was attending Yale Divinity School at the time of her death. She had left Inverness, Scotland, at eighteen for inner-city Cleveland and her memorial service was held at the small Presbyterian church she had attended for almost five decades.

As part of the service, I sang a song whose lyrics included, "They are falling all around me . . . the strongest leaves of my tree." And, later, "but you're not really gonna leave me. . . . It is your path I walk, it is your song I sing, it is your load I take on, it is your air I breathe, it's the record you set that makes me go on, it's your strength that helps me stand, you're not really gonna leave me." And finally, "I will try to sing my song right . . . be sure to let me hear from you." Standing amidst the congregation that had become Grammie's family, nurtured my mom, and blessed my parents' wedding, and to whom I had returned countless times for worship, I bore witness to my deep grief and professed my profound hope. That church and *the* church have been my home and the root of my families for generations.

It was there I learned to love. It was there I learned to connect passionately. And it was there I learned to understand my own body as intimately woven with other bodies to form a collective body.

A third piece that forms the why and how of this work is sewn somewhere between the first two pieces. I was a high school sophomore, he a senior. My best friend had suggested the date because people had begun to wonder if I were lesbian, a thing she deemed terrible. I was there for all the wrong reasons, and I stayed for equally poor ones. I ignored the wisdom of my body, pretended to be interested in the conversation about his sword collection, sat through *A Nightmare on Elm Street* as if I cared, and tried to ask questions and listen to the answers even as none were asked of me. And then there was no escape from the sexual assault that happened in a deserted area. In the years to follow, the silence I kept and the questions of suicide that came were carefully hidden as I threw myself into doing justice for others. Although I could not have formed the words then, my profound and carnal knowledge of colonizing violence propelled me to seek its demise.

These are only three pieces, but they offer a good starting point for the why and how of this work. The church is my home. I was born and bred there and continue to call it my primary community of support and accountability. It was because of my own experience of a passionate, embodied faith that I was drawn into the work of justice in the world. And it was to deepen my faith, express my passion, celebrate my connection to the church, and embolden my justice witness that I was led into seminary and doctoral work in the academy. I am a child of the church, the movement, and the academy.

But I and countless other people and communities, indeed the world and the planet, have been deeply betrayed by a distorted and perverted Christianity. People who inhabit bodies that are poor, queer, female, trans, and genderqueer; people of color; people who live with physical, emotional, and cognitive disabilities; people who practice non-dominant religions or spiritualities; people who are foreigners—as well as the land, animals, water, and air we breathe—have all been abused, exploited, or threatened with destruction in small and large ways in the name of Christianity. Much of the theologizing that has been done has been to support this colonization.

Because of these distortions and perverse purposes, many expressions of the church in North America are in crisis. How to utilize this crisis point as a moment to help the church to reclaim its liberatory, justice-creating presence and practice in the world is one of the questions this book seeks to engage. But how to engage that challenge is not a throw-away question.

Because the church has such a paradoxical legacy and role in the world, the theological task is a complex one. I have found it useful to organize different aspects of this task by means of a matrix designed by Matthew Fox. The points on the matrix are the *Via Positiva*, the *Via*

Negativa, the *Via Creativa,* and the *Via Transformativa.*[1] They translate as the Positive, Negative, Creative, and Transformative Ways. These "paths" offer a method or means by which an individual or community can examine themselves. They offer a way in which individuals or groups can ask questions, understand the world, and determine the best course of spiritual practice and action. Such a matrix is illustrated in Figure 1 below:

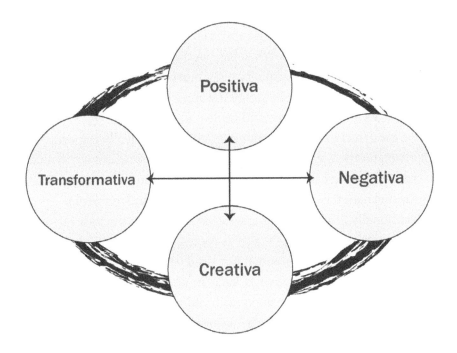

Figure 1

I first used these terms as a way to organize and explore theologically the relationship between our bodies, sexuality, and spirituality in the context of workshops in the local church and in retreat settings.[2] In

1. Matthew Fox, *Original Blessing: A Primer in Creation Spirituality* (New York: Penguin Putnam, 2000), 3.
2. In 1998, I began a three-year process of working with the World Council of Churches US Urban-Rural Mission in a study, action, and reflection process regarding community-based sexuality education. Out of that experience, and in collaboration with my colleague, Fintan Moore, we created a series of workshops known as "Sex and the Spirit" to help participants explore the positive, negative, creative, and transformative aspects of sex, sexuality, and embodiment. I owe a

these settings, this organizational scheme resonated with parishioners and made dialogue more accessible. Repeatedly, I heard that the schema/matrix of Positiva, Negativa, Creativa, and Transformativa "made sense." In my own journey, this matrix has helped me think, pray, and act in more nuanced and complex ways. There are layers, multiple starting points, and different implications of our actions that the Positiva, Negativa, Creativa, Transformativa matrix illustrates plainly.

I find that a matrix with multiple starting and ending points is appropriate for the nuances and complications of embodiment, sexuality, and spirituality. What has been negative, abusive, painful, and destructive about sexuality and embodiment needs to be in dialogue with what has been life-giving and a blessing. One without the other makes for false witness and facile understanding.

But good/bad binaries are not enough either. Equally important is reflection on the ways in which sexuality and embodiment are sources of creativity, procreation, and co-creation with God and can be sources of transformation in the person, the community, and the world.

Additionally, it is not an exaggeration to say that the vast majority of theological writing on sexuality is rooted in cisgender, able-bodied, straight men's experience, which is offered from the dominant cultural perspective. That perspective is valid in and of itself. However, too often it has been distorted, perverted, and passed off as universal and thus colonizing. Because of this, women's and genderqueer people's real bodies, perspectives, and voices are absent from far too many theological conversations.

To move toward addressing this lack, I have sought to include here the stories that nearly 225 women and genderqueer people shared with

---

debt to my World Council of Churches US URM colleagues for much of the conceptual framework employed here. And it was Fintan who first articulated using Fox's four ways as a way to take the journey at the intersections of sexuality and spirituality.

me in the course of my own research.[3] I use these stories as scholars do "primary texts," as a starting place from which to do theology.

Finally, I want to share a fourth quilt piece. I recently helped plan and facilitate a gathering of eighty multifaith justice activists from a variety of religiously based movements. Our aim was to find ways to work together across religious traditions and justice issues. Given the historical moment in which we live—mass incarceration of brown and black people, almost daily stories of police brutality against and killing of people of color, the massacre at Emanuel African Methodist Episcopal Church in Charleston, South Carolina, detention of huge numbers of immigrants in for-profit facilities, deportations of immigrants, and many other examples—we chose to focus the gathering on racial justice. We also knew that for a gathering like this to be successful, we could not simply meet in ways that we often do—talking, discussing, sitting for countless hours in total disregard for our bodies. Instead, we began and ended with different religious leaders taking the group through spiritual practices from their own traditions. We sang and prayed, ritualized, and did art together. And when it came time to begin the action planning, we presented performance pieces from small-group work to set the context into which we would act. One of them involved a litany similar to the following:

Reader One: Tamir Rice
Reader Two: Mia Henderson
Reader Four: Michael Brown
Reader Three: Don't Shoot!

Reader Two: Eric Garner
Reader Three: I can't breathe, I can't breathe . . . [read with pleading]

---

3. I gathered this data in English and Spanish. It was carried out in the field as a Zoomerang survey during April and May of 2012 and contained twenty-seven questions about participants' self-identified race, class, ability, age, sexual orientation, gender identity, and religious affiliation(s) and the ways in which these, individually and collectively, impacted their understanding of their sexuality and their sexual and spiritual practices. For further reference, see Rebecca Voelkel, "Women, Our Bodies and Spirit" (DMin project, United Theological Seminary of the Twin Cities, 2012). While I received 222 completed surveys, nearly 400 women and genderqueer people completed portions of the survey.

Reader Four: Shantel Davis
Reader Three: I don't want to die!

Reader One: Renisha McBride
Reader Three: I want to go home!

Reader Two: Trayvon Martin
Reader Three: [SCREAM]

Reader One: Jordan Davis
Reader Three: [at the same time] I can't breathe, I can't breathe

Reader Four: Kandy Hall
Reader Three: Mom, I'm going to college!

Reader Two: Zoraida Reyes
Reader One: Brittany Stergis
Reader Three: I can't breathe . . . I don't want to die . . . [SCREAM]

It was a profoundly moving and sacred moment. When it was finished, silence and tears were the only response possible. Later, we realized that it had been an experience of prophetic grief made even more intense because Jordan Davis's mother, Lucy McBath, was one of those gathered.

Sitting amongst these religious leaders over the course of three days, I felt myself living in the hybrid space of church-academy-movement. And I also realized again that I inhabit a complex body that calls for nuanced thinking and acting. I was a Christian in a multifaith space whose context included Christian supremacy. I was a white person in a multiracial space whose context included white supremacy. I was a cisgender woman in a multigendered space whose context included sexism and transphobia. I was a lesbian in a space of multiple sexual orientations whose context included homophobia and heterosexism. In short, my body, my social location, and my experience sat at the intersections of privilege and oppression. My legacy is one of benefiting from unspeakable violence and surviving it. My responsibilities include confession, repentance, and repair as well as healing, empowerment, and transformation.

The how and the why of this book, then, are rooted in the complexity of my bodily identity. This complexity reinforces the need for the matrix and the use of the voices of many women and genderqueer people as my primary theological text.[4] My complex body also challenges me to speak in nuanced ways. I am prayerful that I have been able to do so in what follows.

4. Many religions take written words—the Bible, the Qur'an, the Vedanta—to be Holy Scripture, the primary texts from which they take their inspiration. Liberation, feminist, and queer theologies recognize that these written texts originally arose out of and are meant to dialogue with the living word of divine-human experience. Liberation, feminist, and queer theologies especially privilege the experiences of groups that society ignores or disparages. In this book, I have taken the lives and bodies of women and genderqueer people as a primary theological text.

PART I

Via Positiva—The Positive Way

Here's the thing, say Shug. The thing I believe. God is inside you and inside everybody else. You come into the world with God. But only them that search for it inside find it. And sometimes it just manifest itself even if you not looking, or don't know what you looking for. . . .

It? I ask.

Yeah, It. God ain't a he or a she, but a It.

But what do it look like? I ask.

Don't look like nothing, she say. It ain't a picture show. It ain't something you can look at apart from anything else, including yourself. I believe God is everything, say Shug. Everything that is or ever was or ever will be. And when you can feel that, and be happy to feel that, you've found it.[5]

The *Via Positiva* is marked by the good and positive nature, state, and focus of God's gift of creation—particularly of sexuality and embodiment. It describes God's carnal knowledge of creation and creation's returning the favor. It is characterized by the Incarnation and incarnations that bless and are blessed. The *Via Positiva* leads to ever-widening circles of intersectional love, justice, and wholeness —for the individual, community, and society.

5. Alice Walker, *The Color Purple* (Orlando, FL: Harcourt, 2003), 195.

1

God in Creation: Carnal Knowledge

And God stepped out on space,
And He looked around and said,
"I'm lonely—
I'll make me a world."

And far as the eye of God could see
Darkness covered everything,
Blacker than a hundred midnights
Down in a cypress swamp.

Then God smiled,
And the light broke,
And the darkness rolled up on one side,
And the light stood shining on the other,
And God said, *"That's good!"*

Then God reached out and took the light in Her hands,
And God rolled the light around in Her hands
Until She made the sun;
And She set that sun a-blazing in the heavens.
And the light that was left from making the sun
God gathered it up in a shining ball
And flung it against the darkness,
Spangling the night with the moon and stars.
Then down between

The darkness and the light
She hurled the world;
And God said, "*That's good!*"

Then God himself stepped down—
And the sun was on His right hand,
And the moon was on His left;
The stars were clustered about His head,
And the earth was under His feet.
And God walked, and where He trod
His footsteps hollowed the valleys out
And bulged the mountains up.

Then She stopped and looked and saw
That the earth was hot and barren.
So God stepped over to the edge of the world
And She spat out the seven seas;
She batted Her eyes, and the lightnings flashed;
She clapped Her hands, and the thunders rolled;
And the waters above the earth came down,
The cooling waters came down.

Then the green grass sprouted,
And the little red flowers blossomed,
The pine tree pointed his finger to the sky,
And the oak spread out his arms,
The lakes cuddled down in the hollows of the ground,
And the rivers ran down to the sea;
And God smiled again,
And the rainbow appeared,
And curled itself around Her shoulder.

Then God raised Her arm and She waved Her hand
Over the sea and over the land,
And She said, "*Bring forth! Bring forth!*"
And quicker than God could drop Her hand.
Fishes and fowls
And beasts and birds
Swam the rivers and the seas,
Roamed the forests and the woods,
And split the air with their wings.
And God said, "*That's good!*"

Then God walked around,
And God looked around

On all that He had made.
He looked at His sun,
And He looked at His moon,
And He looked at His little stars;
She looked on Her world
With all its living things,
And God said, "*I'm lonely still.*"

Then God sat down
On the side of a hill where She could think;
By a deep, wide river She sat down;
With Her head in Her hands,
God thought and thought,
Till She thought, "*I'll make me a person!*"

Up from the bed of the river
God scooped the clay;
And by the bank of the river
He kneeled Him down;
And there the great God Almighty
Who lit the sun and fixed it in the sky,
Who flung the stars to the most far corner of the night,
Who rounded the earth in the middle of His hand;
This Great God,
Like a mammy bending over her baby,
Kneeled down in the dust
Toiling over a lump of clay
Till He shaped it in His own image;

Then into it She blew the breath of life,
And the person became a living soul.
Amen. Amen.[1]

In one significant part of the Christian theological tradition, special emphasis is placed on the fact that God created the world *ex nihilo* (out of nothing). An important assumption inherent in this assertion is that God is completely and radically "other." Additionally, many theologians of this school suggest that there is no way between God

---

1. James Weldon Johnson, "The Creation," in *The Book of American Negro Poetry* (New York: Harcourt, Brace, 1922), 117–22; adapted with inclusive language for God for use in worship at Spirit of the Lakes United Church of Christ.

and creation because there is an unnavigable gulf between God and that which God created.[2]

But there also exists a strong tradition within Christianity that emphasizes God's immanence in creation, so beautifully articulated by James Weldon Johnson's *The Creation* above. Beginning with nineteenth-century theologian Friedrich Schleiermacher, the liberal theological tradition offers a challenge to the radical otherness of God. In his *Addresses on Religion*, Schleiermacher suggests, "religion is the miracle of direct relationship with the infinite. . . . Religion assumes a desire to lose oneself in the infinite, rather than to preserve one's own finite self."[3] Some scholars from the Religious Society of Friends (Quakers) articulate God's immanence as "that of God" in every person and in all of creation.[4] Many feminist and queer theologians pick up on this liberal theological understanding that God's very essence is present in creation. Rather than wholly other, with no way between the creaturely and the divine because of the absolute gulf between God and humanity, in this part of the Christian theological tradition, God is deeply connected. God recognizes part of God's self in us and we recognize part of ourselves in God. There exists not only a way between creation and the Creator but multiplicities of ways. God and creation share an essence. God and creation share a real relationship. God and creation share a mutual longing for connection. All of these avenues invite intimacy between the Creator and the created.

2. One very clear example of this school of scholarship is Emil Brunner, *The Christian Doctrine of God*, trans. Olive Wyon (Philadelphia: Westminster, 1950), 176.

3. Friedrich Schleiermacher, "Addresses on Religion (1799)," in *A History of Christianity*, ed. Ray C. Petry and Clyde L. Manschreck (Grand Rapids: Baker, 1981), 335–41.

4. George Fox, *The Works of George Fox*, ed. T. H. S. Wallace (State College, PA: New Foundation Publication, George Fox Fund, 1990), 55. This phrase and understanding did not originate with George Fox, the founder of the Religious Society of Friends, but he quoted it widely and it seems to come from his interpretation of the first chapter of Romans. While Fox's understanding of immanence is up for debate, many in the Quaker tradition (particularly those who are now known as "unprogrammed" Friends) have taken it as a central tenet in their theological understanding of God and the creation.

Carnal Knowledge

One way to describe this connection, this shared essence, this real relationship is that God has "carnal knowledge" of humanity. God, in the act of creation, draws from God's own essence and places part of God's self within creation. God knows intimately creation's embodiment. God understands and is in deep relationship with our flesh and bones. God creates in order to be in passionate relationship with creation. "Let us make humankind in our image, according to our likeness," is one way God expresses this carnal relationship.[5] And, in a related way, humanity has carnal knowledge of God—for how could we not, being embodied? We can have some understanding of God's body, God's longings, God's desires because of how God created us. Alice Walker captures some of this in her exquisite theological work, *The Color Purple*.

> Listen, God love everything you love—and a mess of stuff you don't. But more than anything else, God love admiration.
>
> You saying God vain? I ast.
>
> Naw, she say. Not vain, just wanting to share a good thing. I think it pisses god off if you walk by the color purple in a field somewhere and don't notice it.
>
> What it do when it pissed off? I ast.
>
> Oh, it make something else. People think pleasing God is all God care about. But any fool living in the world can see it always trying to please us back.[6]

While many aspects of this carnal knowledge are worth highlighting, I will examine two. The first emerges from the stories that hundreds of women and genderqueer people told me in interviews in the course of research for this book. It is a truth that pertains to the shared essence of Creator and created. The second is also rooted in the answers to my

5. Gen 1:26 NRSV.
6. Walker, *The Color Purple*, 196.

research survey and draws upon early feminist and queer theological wisdom.

Pregnancy and Birth as Co-Creation

Many of my respondents who had gestated a baby commented on the mystical connection they felt with their offspring. As one woman said, "I didn't know I could love like that. It is fierce and protective, overpowering at times." While none would suggest that these were perfect relationships, several respondents commented on the ways in which their children were "flesh of their flesh and bone of their bone." Their children contained some of the women's essence, and the women loved them deeply. Survey respondents also commented on pregnancy and childbirth as an experience of "co-creation" with God. Several suggested that co-creation provided them insight into "how God must feel" and act in relation to humanity and the whole of creation.

This understanding of participating with God in creation—particularly as it pertains to pregnancy and childbirth—springs from a long and proud tradition.[7] The understanding that the experience of motherhood gives us some glimpse into the experience of God is powerful. The story of John Geter, a theologian and pastor who died of AIDS in 1997, offers a powerful example of this.

> I am at home in my own bed. Something is very wrong. I check my temperature and it's 104.2. I call for my mother as the shivers that woke me grow into shakes that feel like a seizure. Without hesitation or embarrassment, Mom lies on top of me, using her weight and her warmth to bring me relief. I know parental metaphors have many dangers, but in this moment I think that if God has only half the sacrificial love for me that my mother and father have, then I can only give thanks and praise.[8]

Geter is right to highlight the dangers of the metaphor of motherhood.

---

7. The tradition of women as co-creators with God is as old as the biblical story with such examples as the birth pangs of the new age, Mary's Magnificat, and the miraculous pregnancies of Sarah, Hannah, and Elizabeth. The co-creation theme runs through much of mujerista, womanist, and feminist writings.
8. Wendy Boring, John A. Geter, and Stefano Penna, "A Maternal Body and a Body with AIDS: Theological Reflections on Carnal Knowledge and the Incarnate God" (paper, annual meeting of the American Academy of Religion, San Francisco, November 24, 1997).

There are significant problems when it is used without nuance or complexity. One of the women who participated in my research nuanced it this way: "For years I would say that I had no body—I was disembodied. This manifest in eating disorders and self-harm behaviors. Now I am working to come more here into my body. Becoming a biological mother helped—it added nuance and language to my body that I appreciated. Within it, I still sometimes struggle with the virgin/mother/whore triad of Christianity but, as I age, I am getting better at bringing it all together."[9]

In this context, I only want to highlight the notion that the acts of giving birth and nurturing offspring are deeply carnal experiences, rooted in the body. Because they are related to and connected with the act of creation, they can offer some revelation into God's experiences and relationships and they provide a challenge to the theological assertion of God's radical otherness.

Using the stories of women and genderqueer people as a primary source of theological understanding, we see pregnancy and childbirth as a sharing of essence and form that creates a bond of love and connection. Such experience provides a compelling argument for the immanence of God, for God's carnal knowledge of humanity, and for God's body knit throughout creation. It is important to note, however, that co-creation does not imply a conflict-free, naïve, simplistic connection between God and creation. Carnal knowledge is deep and true knowledge, flesh-and-bones knowledge.

> There is an alien living inside my body. . . . I am so sick, I want to die. I know it is a baby, and I know I'm supposed to feel love, but right now all I feel is fear and the certainty that there isn't a maternal bone in my body. . . . The pain comes on in waves, wave after wave of paralyzing pain. I am pinned by pain, with no escape. Pinned down by pain. . . . I feel like a milk wagon. All I do is nurse. My brain is fuzzy, my body a wreck. I can't remember the last time I took a shower. I didn't think it was possible to feel this tired, this resentful, this fragmented, this alive.[10]

9. Rebecca Voelkel, "Women, Our Bodies and Spirit" (DMin project, United Theological Seminary of the Twin Cities, 2012).
10. Boring, Geter, and Penna, "A Maternal Body."

God and Humanity as "Lovers"

The second aspect of the connection and intimacy between God and creation takes the above understanding of love and deepens it. It highlights the more sexual and sensual understandings of "carnal knowledge." Much of the scriptural witness highlights, illustrates, and cajoles the faithful to love. God's invitation in creation is to love. And our first and most faithful response is to act as lover—of God and of the world.[11]

> When the Pharisees heard that he had silenced the Sadducees, they gathered together, and one of them, a lawyer, asked him a question to test him. "Teacher, which commandment in the law is the greatest?" He said to him, "'You shall love the Lord your God with all your heart, and with all your soul, and with all your mind.' This is the greatest and first commandment. And a second is like it: 'You shall love your neighbor as yourself.' On these two commandments hang all the law and the prophets."[12]

God in the world is love and lover; our response to God in the world, to one another, and to creation is as lover. While on the one hand, this is a common understanding of God and of humanity, the use of the word "lover" adds an explicitly sexual connotation. Moreover, it introduces an underlying precept of many queer and feminist theologians (and many of the women and genderqueer people who participated in my research) that embodiment and sexuality are at the foundation of God's good act in creation. One of the women who participated in my research articulated it this way:

> My experience as a white, upper middle class, Protestant, educated person from the South led me to have not much understanding of myself as a sexual being and certainly not a relationship between my sexuality and my spirituality. I understood that I was attractive to boys and then men. I did not connect that with spirituality in any sense until I fell in love with my high school sweetheart (a boy). We were both people of faith and I felt the Godliness of our relationship. Later as an adult, I knew when

11. Carter Heyward, "Sexuality, Love and Justice," in *Weaving the Visions: New Patterns in Feminist Spirituality*, ed. Judith Plaskow and Carol P. Christ (New York: Harper & Row, 1989), 293.
12. Matt 22:34–40 NRSV.

relationships were real when I felt spirituality in them. In my relationship with my wife, I feel complete in the sense that I am who I am supposed to be and that we are living a blessed and Godly life. I know I am in God's image and that our love is wonderfully right.[13]

This image of God as lover challenges a deeply held belief in some parts of Christianity: that of the nonsexuality of God. Part 2 will more deeply deal with the ways in which the metaphor of God's carnal knowledge of creation is suppressed, but it is important to note the ways in which an understanding of God with carnal knowledge disrupts oppression. It disrupts oppression because so many oppressive systems are rooted in the theological assertion that God is nonsexual. In this oppression-supporting system, God has no sexual partner (as contrasted with the gods and goddesses of pagan mythology). Furthermore, there is a connection between the nonsexuality of God and exclusively male images for God. This maleness and nonsexuality of God is used, in turn, to control sexuality in general and that of women and genderqueer people in particular. This connection emerges when the image of God is threatened by female metaphors. As Judith Plaskow observes, "Resistance to female images for God stems not only from the fact that they alter the gender of God but also from their threatening God with sexuality."[14]

Another way in which God's carnal knowledge of and deep connection with creation disrupts oppression is through the explicit understanding of erotic power. Erotic power deepens and more fully explicates the understanding of God as lover and our vocation as creative lovers in return. The word "erotic" comes from the Greek word *eros*. *Eros* is both love and desire, but it is also deeply connected to the capacity to be creative. One of God's gifts to creation, one of the ways in which we are able to respond to God as lover, is through erotic power. I will talk more about both the importance of desire and the explicitly sexual nature of erotic power later in this chapter and in part 3. For now, it is simply important to highlight that intrinsic to the

---

13. Voelkel, "Women, Our Bodies and Spirit."

14. Judith Plaskow, *Standing Again at Sinai: Judaism from a Feminist Perspective* (San Francisco: Harper & Row, 1990), 187.

Via Positiva is erotic power, the carnally rooted, enfleshed capacity to act creatively in love.

Sexuality

The above exploration strengthens and informs the definition of sexuality that I employ in this work. Drawn from the work of theologians Sandra Longfellow and James Nelson, sexuality is "the Divine invitation to find our destinies not in loneliness, but in deep connection."[15] Sexuality, then, is one way that God invites our intimacy with God and with one another. It is one expression of the carnal knowledge we share with God. It is one expression of erotic power. This divine invitation has implications for our bodies, but it is broader than our physical selves. It suggests a deep connection between sexuality and spirituality, between our bodies and our spirits. It suggests that our deepest longings for connection—sexually, spiritually, physically—are intertwined and a gift from God. However, it is important that sexuality and embodiment are not decontextualized or romanticized. That is to say, God's good act in creation requires an intimate interweaving of embodiment, sexuality, love, and justice.

When I was a child with the crush I describe in the introduction, it was my sexuality that drew me to Melissa Gilbert and that, in turn, drew me toward Jean Donovan, Bishop Romero, and liberation theology. Sexuality, then, is what draws us to make love and justice in the world. It invites us to manifest erotic power. It draws and drives us toward another person. It urges and compels us into deeper connections, deeper bonds. It is deeply personal and expressed between lovers. But it is also what draws the artist toward passionate acts of creativity; the parent toward a child in ways that are relentlessly life-sharing and transcend exhaustion; and drives the revolutionary whose deepest desire is for her people. Cornel West says that "just as justice is what love looks like in public and tenderness is what love feels like in private, deep democratic revolution is what

15. James B. Nelson and Sandra P. Longfellow, eds., *Sexuality and the Sacred: Sources for Theological Reflection* (Louisville: Westminster John Knox, 1994), xiv.

justice looks like in practice."[16] Sexuality, then, is deeply intertwined with justice.[17]

An example of the inseparability of sexuality, love, and justice comes from the Stonewall riots, which birthed the modern LGBTQ movement.

> They were queer, every one of them. . . . They were drag queens and bull dykes. They were Black and white, Latino and Asian American and they were mostly working class and poor.
>
> They had been beaten up, scorned by their families as repulsive, committed to mental hospitals. Their lives were filled with fear, intimidation and shame.
>
> But on this night in the summer of 1969, something happened. . . . They recognized, they perceived, something about themselves and one another. They saw the holy in their midst, or at least the evidence of holiness which is dignity and, so awakened, they claimed an erotic power.
>
> At first it was according to the script. The police entered the bar; the mafia bosses took their things and left; and the queers were herded out the door.
>
> But as they were being pushed toward the usual, normal humiliation, something shifted. Some energy changed. And someone stopped. Someone was overcome by the Spirit and said, no, not this time. And before they knew it, coins were being thrown—a symbol of the system of extortion.
>
> And soon the paddy wagon had been emptied and the police pushed back into the bar.
>
> And like the collective expression of love in public, word went around Christopher Street and Greenwich Village and the crowds gathered. And over the course of the next five nights, they swelled and swelled.
>
> In response, the tactical police force was called in and, with their billy clubs and riot gear, they pushed into the crowd.
>
> But the crowd would not be quashed. Instead, when the tactical police force came at them, they ran ahead, turned the block and re-formed behind the police.

16. Cornel West, "A Love Supreme," *The Occupied Wall Street Journal*, November 18, 2011, http://tinyurl.com/hn7srrq.
17. Heyward, "Sexuality, Love and Justice," 295.

When the police whirled around to reverse direction at one point, they found themselves face-to-face with their worst nightmare: a chorus line of mocking queens, their arms clasped around each other, kicking their heels in the air Rockettes-style and singing at the tops of their sardonic voices:

"We are the Stonewall girls
We wear our hair in curls
We wear no underwear
We show our pubic hair . . .
We wear our dungarees
Above our nelly knees!"

It was a deliciously witty, creative counterpoint to the tactical police force's brute force. It was a claiming of embodied, erotic love. It was a yes to their love for themselves, for one another. They chose music and laughter, resistance and creativity, life and love and dignity in who and whose they were.[18]

Part 2 will explore in more depth the implications of an absence of justice and the ways in which systemic injustices mar, injure, and can destroy God's good gift of creation. However, for this section, it is important to begin with the *Via Positiva* of claiming God's gift of embodiment and sexuality. And it is impossible to talk about God's gift of embodiment and sexuality without talking about justice and love and the ways in which they are intertwined. Additionally, our understanding of sexuality is not isolated to genital expression. While sexual, genital expression is a good and blessed part of sexuality, I employ a broader understanding of sexuality. Sexuality is our embodied desire to connect with God and one another in just and loving ways.

Longing, Desire, and Pleasure as Part of God's Gift

Inherent in God's gift of embodiment and sexuality is the reality that longing, desire, and pleasure can be important ways in which God communicates with creation. Although distorted by systems of

---

18. Rebecca Voelkel, "Highlander Singers, Jesus Challengers and Outrageous Street Dancers," (sermon, Bishops and Elders Council Meeting, Dallas, TX, September 10, 2006).

oppression and suspect by many Christians, desire, longing, and pleasure can lead both the individual and the community into deeper relationship with God and with one another.[19] The psalmist articulates this well, "O God, you are my God, earnestly I seek you; my soul thirsts for you, my flesh longs for you."[20] The writer of the Song of Solomon testifies, "I am my beloved's, and his desire is for me."[21] And more explicitly,

I slept, but my heart was awake.
Listen! My beloved is knocking.
"Open to me, my sister, my love, my dove, my perfect one;
for my head is wet with dew,
my locks with the drops of the night."
I had put off my garment;
how could I put it on again?
I had bathed my feet;
how could I soil them?
My beloved thrust a hand into the opening,
and my innermost being yearned.[22]

Longing, desire, and pleasure are critical components in the *Via Positiva*. They can be one way in which God communicates with humanity. What we long for and desire—particularly over the long haul—can be God-given evidence of vocation. What brings us deep pleasure can be confirmation of our truest selves. Particularly in the context of oppression—when systems of power dictate that a person is less valuable than another or that a group of people are categorically unworthy of dignity—longing, desire, and pleasure can be the way God communicates to those people what is just and right. Part 3 will cover this in much more detail, but longing and desire often populate our dreams—both during the day and when we are asleep; we often dream the world we may not be experiencing in the now. This dreaming is

19. For a definition of colonization, see the glossary. One survey respondent articulated the ways in which some Christian churches problematize the body, "[we were taught] the body can interfere with our spiritual growth, if we do not feed the spirit."
20. Ps 63:1 NASB.
21. Song 7:10 NRSV. All scriptural citations are taken from the New Revised Standard Version unless otherwise indicated.
22. Song 5:2–4.

a crucial part of the justice-making process. And at its core is that for which we long and desire, that which brings us pleasure and joy. This interaction between two white, queer, working-poor women is a profound example of this.

> What I offered my friend was the dangerous revelation of desire. I began a sentence with "I want," and we both blushed and looked around. I told Amber: I want to write a great book—I want to make a difference—I want to have adventures and take enormous risks and be everything they say we are and not give a damn what anyone says. . . . Saying "I want" and meaning it was more dangerous for us than naming our various sexual adventures. Revolutions begin when people look each other in the eyes, say "I want," and mean it.[23]

Several years ago, I had a conversation with a woman on an airplane. She had noticed that I was wearing a National LGBTQ Task Force polar fleece and asked me about it. When I responded that I was the Faith Work Director, she began a conversation that lasted the rest of the flight. She asked me detailed questions about scripture and its role in my life. It was a lively conversation. The heart of the matter for her was my assertion that God communicated with us through our desires and longings and that LGBTQ people's coming-out processes were a response to God's call. She challenged me that responding to longings and desires was tantamount to "giving in" to an addiction and represented a "slippery slope." She said that "allowing" men to have sex with men would be immediately followed by allowing adults to have sex with children and with animals and other abusive situations. She believed that we needed to control these "wanton desires" as a mark of disciplined discipleship.

This very common perspective suggests that the faithful Christian life is best articulated by Mark 9:43: "If your hand causes you to stumble, cut it off; it is better for you to enter life maimed than to have two hands and to go to hell, to the unquenchable fire." In this perspective, desire, longing, and pleasure are to be repressed and amputated. But it is critically important to differentiate between

---

23. Dorothy Allison, foreword to *My Dangerous Desires: A Queer Girl Dreaming Her Way Home*, by Amber Hollibaugh (Durham, NC: Duke University Press, 2000), xii–xiii.

addiction, obsession, and hedonism on the one hand and longing, desire, and pleasure on the other.

For this work, the critical distinction lies in the use of power. God as lover, filled with carnal knowledge of creation, uses erotic power in order to create empowered subjects who use their own erotic power to further justice and love in the world. This is very different from a nonsexual God operating in a world in which "the flesh" is suspect as a locus of sin and temptation. Such a suspicion of embodiment has its roots in a history of colonization.

While I will discuss this in much more depth in part 2, it is important to note here the ways in which oppression has utilized "the flesh." There are many examples of this within Christianity, but perhaps none as important as Augustine. Utilizing the Greek philosophical tradition, particularly Neoplatonism, Augustine understood that there was an essential difference between spirit and flesh, that spirit was better than flesh and therefore ought to subordinate flesh. Western Christian orthodoxy turned this hierarchical model of human nature into a patriarchal social model. Male, and men, go with spirit and reason, while menstruating, childbearing, lactating females are mired in flesh and blood. What could be more natural than for males to subordinate females? The model has been generalized, with the powers that be identifying themselves with spirit and reason and defining oppressed classes as more governed by, or limited by, the flesh and thus sin prone.[24] Native peoples were identified by Christian, European colonizers as more defined by "the flesh" and, therefore, as savages.[25]

---

24. Rosemary Radford Ruether (*Sexism and God-talk: Toward a Feminist Theology* [Boston: Beacon Press, 1983]) and other early feminist theologians do a very helpful job in exposing "patriarchal anthropology" found in Augustine and elaborated upon by Thomas Aquinas, Martin Luther, and Karl Barth, to name just a few. These men drew heavily from earlier Greek philosophy, which suggested a chain of being that correlated to a chain of power and command: God-spirits-male-female-nonhuman-nature-matter. This led them to purport that women were subordinate, under the domination of men. Ruether (*Sexism and God-talk*, 95), citing Augustine's *De Trinitate* 7.7.10, suggests, "Although Augustine concedes woman's redeemability and hence her participation in the image of God, it is so overbalanced by her bodily representation of inferior, sin-prone self that he regards her as possessing the image of God only secondarily."

25. Joey L. Mogul, Andrea J. Ritchie, and Kay Whitlock, eds., *Queer (In)justice: The Criminalization of LGBT People in the United States* (Boston: Beacon Press, 2011), 1–5. Perhaps the most vicious and deadly evidence of this understanding is the Doctrine of Discovery. A series of fifteenth-century papal bulls (official statements by the Pope) came to be known as the Doctrine of Discovery and

The earth, first identified as female, was to be controlled, raped, and pillaged for its resources. It is important to emphasize the connection between the nonsexual, distant, male, monotheistic God and a suspicion of "the flesh" and its longing, desire, and pleasure.

It is critical to understand longing, desire, and pleasure in the context of God as a lover with carnal knowledge of and deeply connected to creation. Longing, desire, and pleasure are markers of shared erotic power, while addiction, obsession, and hedonism are examples of distorted power. Addiction locates power outside of ourselves and is by definition disempowering of the one addicted. Obsession seeks to use power over others, objectifying and disempowering the object of the obsession. Hedonism seeks to make pleasure the ultimate end, ignoring relationship and justice as God's gifts.

In part 2 I will explore the ways in which longing, desire, and pleasure can be distorted into addiction, obsession, and hedonism through the forces of oppression and colonization. However, when God's gifts of longing, desire, and pleasure draw us into deeper connections where love and justice are embodied, we can glimpse the face of God.

gave Christian explorers the right to claim lands they "discovered" and lay claim to those lands for their Christian monarchs. Any land that was not inhabited by Christians was available to be "discovered," claimed, and exploited. If the "pagan" inhabitants could be converted, they might be spared. If not, they could be enslaved or killed.

2

Incarnation and Incarnations

I love my body. . . .[1]

. . . Recently upon reflection during a study of a Biblical text, I realized how extremely grateful I am for my body and the experiences it has allowed me to have. Athletics, travel, physical activities, childbirth. This awareness led me to see my body as something entirely positive, powerful and functional. I also felt extremely grateful for this new perspective. . . .[2]

I pass very, very well. I am extremely grateful. It is a joy! I sometimes have some survivor guilt because so many women of gender experience never get to experience it. As for my body, after waiting so long for my breasts, I really love them. They feel good and they are that outward, obvious symbol of femaleness. I feel good to look like all the other girls. . . . I love my skin on hormones, so soft. . . .[3]

I love my breasts! The way they fit perfectly in the cup of my hand. How they're full and heavy with perfect nipples. I love other women's breasts and wonder if I'll ever be able to experience them pressed against me.[4]

---

1. These are quotations from women I interviewed for my DMin thesis, "Women, Our Bodies and Spirit."
2. Ibid.
3. Ibid.
4. Ibid.

At its core, the Christian claim that God took on human flesh as a mode of revelation and blessing has radical implications for humanity. Many feminist, queer, and liberation theologians root their work in this core Christian understanding of incarnation. God's incarnation and the relationship of God's body to human bodies provides inspiration and guidance to many who work for embodied justice.[5]

According to the Christian doctrine of incarnation, God chose to fully experience the reality of living in a human body, completely enfleshed. This doctrine is central to my understanding of the carnal relationship between God and creation. However, the understanding of incarnation is weakened by traditional implications that God is first and "really" spirit, rather than flesh. I do not affirm this Neoplatonic dualism, nor the ways in which Christian orthodoxy has used this dualism to perpetrate and justify oppression of whole classes of people identified more closely with "the flesh." Instead, I hold that God's essence is both intimately known to and experienced by the creation, and far beyond our wildest imaginings. Because God's mystery surpasses human experience, incarnation is a powerful form of revelation that speaks to the abundance of God's embodied love in ways that allow for deep knowledge and understanding of God. Incarnation reveals God but does not limit God.[6]

Furthermore, according to the witness of the canonical Gospels, God incarnate in the person of Jesus of Nazareth lived under an occupation by Rome, touched and was touched by those with illness, interacted with those marginalized by culture and religion, challenged systems of injustice, and died the death of a political prisoner. God incarnate in the person of Jesus of Nazareth experienced not only what it felt like to live enfleshed but what it felt like to live enfleshed in that paradoxical social location of holding power and privilege (as a Jewish male and rabbi) and experiencing oppression and suffering (as a subject of

---

5. Laurel Schneider, "Promiscuous Incarnation," in *The Embrace of Eros: Bodies, Desires, and Sexuality in Christianity*, ed. Margaret D. Kamitsuka (Minneapolis: Fortress Press, 2010), 231.
6. God is incarnate and embodied in the energetic forces that quantum physicists study, in the "music of the stars" of which poets such as Madeleine L'Engle have written, and in the very forces of evolution, plate tectonics, and other forces that are not human incarnation or embodiment but are embodied nonetheless.

Rome). Because of this, many liberation theologians have pointed to the incarnation as one of the most radical resources within Christianity.

Womanist theologian Delores Williams speaks of the "solidarity of the cross." Incarnation means not that a spiritual God decided to put on matter for a while but that God incarnate in the person of Jesus chose to live a life with the poor and marginalized, resisting oppression and working for justice. Because of the kind of life Jesus led, and the systems of oppression in which he lived it, he was arrested, tried, and executed by the religious and political authorities of his day. This narrative shows that God is radically with us and for us. Because of what God did in the person and life of Jesus, God stands in solidarity with any person or people oppressed or marginalized by religious, economic, or political authorities. Such is the meaning of the incarnation and the cross.[7]

The incarnation, then, is a powerful way in which God has carnal knowledge of humanity, carnal knowledge that is rooted in justice, solidarity, and liberation. But God did not take on human form in order to understand and love only first-century Palestinian Jewish men (the particular body and social location Jesus is reported to have inhabited). Instead, the incarnation has been used to illustrate God's love for all of humanity. God became embodied in order to have a human experience, in order to become intimate with us, in order to hallow the body.[8] The incarnation is both an act of intimacy between God and humanity and a blessing of all of our incarnations.

But this incarnation is not exclusive or narrow. Instead, as theologian Laurel Schneider suggests, the incarnation is promiscuous. Promiscuous means that God is not forming a covenant with just one individual or, for that matter, just one race or nation. God desires to have many covenant partners, not only individuals but whole communities, too. God in the person of Jesus seeks to love many at the same time.

7. Delores Williams, "Re-Imagining Jesus" (lecture, "Re-Imagining: A Global Theological Conference by Women: For Men and Women," Minneapolis, November 5, 1993).
8. Schneider, "Promiscuous Incarnation," 231–46.

This promiscuity of God's embodiment and love interrupts competition, jealousy, and exceptionalism. God's attention and resources are boundless and extravagant. What one person or community "gets" does not diminish or take away from the depth of relationship and carnal connection between God and another, nor does God's love and covenant with one person or people mean that they are chosen or more important than others. There is enough of God's love to go around with an abundance left over. God's faithfulness is a matter not of God's having no other partners but us, but of God's reliability in being for us, supportive of us, and creatively engaged with us. God is worthy of our trust not because God loves only us but because God loves us fully and abundantly.

The use of "promiscuous" in this way is vintage queer scholarship. Queering promiscuous—using it in unconventional ways, pairing it with "incarnation" in order to upend the meaning of both—opens up the possibility of multiple covenants, destabilizes our categories of faithfulness, and refocuses our attention away from a singular emphasis on an individual relationship with God and toward the importance of God's relationship with the communal body. God's promiscuous incarnation desires a deeper intimacy and a new covenant with humanity that is based on shared carnal experience and knowing—with the individual bodies and with the communal body.

Another reason for reconceptualizing incarnation as promiscuous in the queered sense is the strong historical connection between monogamy and ownership of women's bodies and reproductive capabilities. In patrilineal societies, where property inheritance is passed through the father, clear identification of a child's paternity is paramount. In the absence of DNA testing, control of women's sexual activity became the primary means of ensuring paternity. Thus, sexual control of women's bodies and sexual expression became tied to social order. Because patrilineality is the dominant traditional form of familial organization in early Christian, Jewish, and Muslim societies, this may account for the deep connections between owning and controlling women's sexuality and monotheistic religious understandings of sexual morality.[9] To interrupt the connection between patriarchal ownership and control of women's bodies, that which is promiscuous connotes extravagance, justice, and liberated bodies.[10]

Furthermore, God's promiscuous longing and desire to know and be intimate with humanity suggests that the incarnation blesses all our incarnations. God's incarnation blesses all of creation, making human bodies sacred—and that means *all* bodies. Rooted in the liberation tradition, this promiscuous incarnation and hallowing of all incarnations is particularly important for bodies of color, poor bodies, women's bodies, and transgender and genderqueer bodies, which have been literally desecrated, dissected, and destroyed. In my research, many women and genderqueer people noted the importance of hallowing their own bodies. The four quotes with which I began this chapter illustrate the importance of the *Via Positiva* and the important role that the incarnation's blessing of our incarnations can have.

However, this hallowing of bodies cannot be done without further nuance. It is important to state explicitly that there is no universal experience of incarnation. In order to walk the *Via Positiva* and claim the blessing and gift of embodiment and incarnation, we need to speak of particular people and specific bodies. We need to explore the ways that most of us have multiple identities and live at the intersections of communities.[11] There must be space for hallowing, honoring, and empowering "real bodies . . . fleshy, flesh."[12] Additionally, there must be recognition that the experience of the blessing of embodiment and sexuality as gifts from God varies depending upon race, class, age, ability, sexual orientation, gender identity, and many other differences in culture and religious context. Indeed, the particular intersections

---

9. Schneider, "Promiscuous Incarnation," 235–36.
10. It is worth noting that polygamy and a queered sense of promiscuity are very different. At issue is the ownership and control of women's bodies and sexuality. Polygamous relationships, particularly those in ancient Near East societies, were not promiscuous in the sense I am using it here.
11. Kimberlé W. Crenshaw, "Mapping the Margins: Intersectionality, Identity Politics, and Violence against Women of Color," *Stanford Law Review* 43, no. 6 (1991): 1241–99. See the definition of intersectionality in the glossary.
12. Schneider, "Promiscuous Incarnation," 242.

of these identities create a variety of experiences and, therefore, incarnations and theological lenses.

It is impossible to separate one's experience of one's body from the particularities of that body. This is true of all our particularities. "As African Americans and other peoples of color particularly know, race affects one's experience and even embodiment of gender."[13] The corollary is also true: gender affects one's experience and even embodiment of race. Furthermore, how age, ability, race, class, or any other determinant of our experience shape one's experience is very much a function of one's social and cultural context. The experience of being African American in Alabama is different than in Minnesota. Being LGBTQ as a white person is different from being same-gender loving as a person of color. Ability, age, sexual orientation, class, and other particularities of embodiment are impacted by the systems of injustice and culture in which they are experienced, affect one another, and create a particular theological lens. Two examples illustrate this point.

One woman I interviewed shared with me that as an African American woman, she felt very affirmed and loved because of her weight. She said in her cultural context, curves, big breasts, and large buttocks were considered sexy. She noted how her white women friends often strove to lose weight in order to be sexy and how differently she experienced her body and its weight than they did. However, she also noted that she and many other African American women struggled with health issues because of being overweight. For her, the intersection of class, race, and the blessing of embodiment was a complex one. She said, "nothing is complete gift, nothing is complete curse."[14]

This was nuanced further in a conversation with two Puerto Rican

13. Laurel Schneider, "What Race Is Your Sex?," in *Disrupting White Supremacy from Within: White People on What We Need to Do*, ed. Jennifer Harvey, Karin A. Case, and Robin Hawley Gorsline (Cleveland, OH: Pilgrim Press, 2004), 142.
14. As I shared in the introduction, this book seeks to hold the blessing of embodiment and sexuality in conversation with the realities of colonization, oppression, and mortality, as well as the opportunities for creativity and transformation. This woman's reflection points to the need for a matrix when examining embodiment and sexuality.

sisters. One was tall, small breasted, almost skinny, and light skinned; the other was taller, with large buttocks, big breasts, and darker skin. As they spoke with me, they reflected on their experiences of living on the island of Puerto Rico and living in the continental United States. When they were in Puerto Rico, the darker, more voluptuous sister was considered beautiful and received a lot of sexual attention. When they were in the continental United States, the lighter, thinner, more sculpted sister was considered beautiful and received the attention. They spoke about the impact of external factors on their self-perceptions and their relationships with their own bodies. For both, their internal sense of beauty and blessing had to be cultivated in conversation with culture and context.

For these three women, and most of those women and genderqueer people who participated in my research, the cultural context and the presence of the systemic oppression in which they lived directly impacted how they experienced the gift of embodiment and their particular incarnation. Some things were pluses in one culture and minuses in another culture because different cultures have different aesthetics and different systems of power and oppression. For these women and genderqueer people, their bodies and their experiences of sexuality were complicated—gift and source of pain and suffering.

Community as Locus of Incarnation, Support, and Accountability

As we examine the interaction between a promiscuous incarnation and our particular and specific incarnations, another facet that bears more explicit emphasis is the importance of community. Starting with the apostle Paul's connection between Jesus's incarnation and the early Christian community as "the Body of Christ" (1 Corinthians 12), Christian theologians have emphasized community as a marker of faithful Christian life. Feminist theologian Rita Nakashima Brock recognizes this emphasis on community but challenges and nuances it when she aims to develop "a christology not centered in Jesus, but in relationship and community as the whole-making, healing center of Christianity." She names this "Christa/Community."[15] It is the

Christian community, in which Jesus plays a central role but that he does not control, that truly reveals divine incarnation and the power to save. In Christa/Community there is erotic power within connectedness. The erotic power of community resides in the connectedness, not in any single individual.[16]

Any theological examination of bodies requires two foci: the bodies themselves and that which connects them. God's carnal relationship with humanity is both with the individual, particular, contextualized body and with the collective body. But we need one more level of complexity because God also has a carnal relationship with the body of Christ gathered in a particular community. Speaking of the incarnation as promiscuous highlights the fact that God enters into deep, enfleshed, erotic covenant with a multiplicity of communal bodies/ bodies politic. There are a multiplicity of covenants and many of them are with communal bodies. Humanity's vocation as lover does not only reside in an individual but draws that individual into relationships of justice and love with other individuals and with the community. Any description of the *Via Positiva*, and any theological construction that takes seriously embodiment and sexuality, must recognize a complex relationship between the individual and the community. This is true both for the pastoral needs of the individual and the health of the community *and* for the theological honesty of this work.

But it is equally important to avoid naïve valorizing of community. Communities can be wholesome and lifegiving, but they can also be dysfunctional and oppressive—sometimes both at once. The *Via Positiva* must be modified and in conversation with the *Via Negativa* because the realities of betrayal, systems of domination and oppression, and

---

15. Rita Nakashima Brock, *Journeys by Heart: A Christology of Erotic Power* (New York: Crossroad, 1988), 55. Brock writes, "as I recall, the first use of the term Christa was in reference to the crucifix in the Cathedral of Saint John the Divine in New York City. The Christ on the crucifix, labeled Christa, was female. In using Christa instead of Christ, I am using a term that points away from a sole identification of Christ with Jesus. In combining it with community, I want to shift the focus of salvation away from heroic individuals, male or female. I agree with Nelle Morton, in *The Journey Is Home* (Boston: Beacon Press, 1985), 194–98, that new realities must be accompanied by metaphors that shatter old, conventional ways of thinking and usher in new images. Using the term Christa/ Community affirms my conviction about the sacredness of community."

16. Brock, *Journeys by Heart*, 55.

relationships marked by violence can be present within any communal context. I will explore these in more depth in part 2.

PART II

Via Negativa—The Negative Way

The *Via Negativa* is characterized by that which colonizes. It is the part of the theological matrix that looks at the forces of sin, crucifixion, and their supporting theological hegemonies. The *Via Negativa* focuses on devastation, targeted violence, degradation, and that which creates conditions of despair and how we confront these in critical, analytical, and courageous ways.

> The smells here . . . all bring me back to my younger self, a very defiant, angry, terrified, teenage lesbian stripper. . . .
>
> I was dancing in a cage, the go-go stripper kind, dancing to Otis Redding, dancing hard. One man would not stay back, kept reaching into the cage trying to catch my feet and ankles, kept putting twenty-dollar bills into the cage. And I kept kicking them out. A set was fifteen minutes, no stops onstage; then they would open up the back of the cage and you'd come hurtling out and down the steep back stairs into the dressing room. This guy had been out front all night, getting drunker, waiting for each of my sets, then pushing the money through the bars as he grabbed for my feet.
>
> I was tired. It was my next to last set, and I'd had it up to here with him, with his money and his fingers. Finally, I took his money and started to build it into my routine—rubbing it on my body, moving it between my legs. He kept putting more twenties on the stage, money he thought guaranteed him my time, my body, after the music ended. He kept putting twenties there until I had a stack of them in my hands.

Slowly I ripped every fucking twenty-dollar bill up into tiny pieces and sprinkled them outside the cage over his head while he screamed about whores, about cock teasers, about me. Then he left. At least that's what I thought.

When I came out for my last set he was nowhere around. I danced that fifteen minutes so tired I came off the stage not even looking down to see the stairs. Too bad. He'd broken glass and spread it on each of the steps leading to the back room. I hit that glass going a hundred. It split my feet apart before I could stop, pounded it deep inside the creases. I almost bled to death.

All day I've been thinking of that time, remembering being that young, that tired, that angry, that scared, that lonely. Thinking about power and about lacking it.[1]

1. Hollibaugh, *My Dangerous Desires*, 1.

3

Colonization and Sin

In part 1, I expanded on embodiment and sexuality as gift and blessing. However, in much the same way that Christian theology asserts that an understanding of resurrection is impossible without an understanding of crucifixion, any theological construction that takes women's and genderqueer people's embodiment and sexuality seriously must speak honestly of colonization. By colonization, I mean the context and process by which one group of people employ power and resources to subjugate, oppress, marginalize, and/or kill another group or groups of people, the land, and its creatures. In colonization, economic, religious, political, cultural, and relational systems of power are deeply intertwined and infused with an ethic of power-over, violence, extraction for profit, scarcity, use, and a subject/object perspective. That is to say, colonization demands the subduing of the object. In this use of the term colonization, there is a strong link between "empire"/imperialism and colonization that perpetuates colonizer/colonized relationships.

The story above is a potent metaphor for the reality and power of colonization. The young dancer is physically within a cage. The purpose of the cage is exploitive. She is confined, held, contained, and controlled. The stalker is trying to grab, take, and possess her. He believes he has the right to do so because of all he has been taught. And when she acts in defiance, dancing her own dance, refusing the money, and then tearing it up—in many ways remarkable acts given the reality of the cage of colonization in which she lives—she is cut down and almost bleeds to death. This story illustrates the colonization itself, the systems of belief (hegemonies, including theological hegemonies) that support and perpetuate it and the acts of violence that reestablish and maintain the hierarchies that are the markers of colonization.

The Cage: Domination, Hierarchies, and Binaries

Historical colonization on the North American continent—largely established and perpetrated by European, able-bodied, heterosexual, cisgender, white, Christian men at the behest of wealthy colonizers (i.e., royalty, business owners, and church officials)—resulted in a context of colonization that is still very much present in the United States today. This historical colonization combined the forces of economic, cultural, and religious powers from Europe that came to the Americas (and elsewhere) to conquer, extract, convert, and enrich. This onslaught centered power in the colonizer (the soldier, the priest, the business owner—whose differences became almost inconsequential in the act of colonizing). The "New World" and its millions of people, animals, and resources were objects upon which violent power was perpetrated in order to serve the needs and wants of the colonizer.

This system of dominance and submission, spread by the sword and gun, was radically different from the cultures the colonizers encountered. But because it was predicated on a colonizing mindset, the encounter with difference only served to reinforce the colonizing world view. Indeed, the encounter with difference elicited the powerful impulse to compel an establishment of "proper" hierarchies rooted in dominance and submission. As one Franciscan wrote in 1775:

Among the women I saw some men dressed like women, with whom they go about regularly, never joining the men. . . . From this I inferred they must be hermaphrodites, but from what I learned later I understood that they were sodomites, dedicated to nefarious practices. From all the foregoing I conclude that in this matter of incontinence there will be much to do when the Holy Faith and the Christian religion are established among them.[1]

Implicit in this system of hierarchies rooted in dominance and submission is an understanding of binaries. In order to differentiate between what is dominant and what is submissive, in order to establish appropriate hierarchies, systems of colonization rely upon binaries. In the diary excerpt above, the Franciscan Pedro Font was deeply troubled by what he understood as sodomy. Whether he was encountering a practice of a "third sex" or "two-spirit," both the gender and supposed sexual practices of those individuals constituted "incontinence" for him because they violated the binary of "men/women" and the hierarchal power that he presumed each connoted. Additional binaries upon which historical colonization of the Americas relied included heathen/Christian and savage/civilized. Sometimes the binary was used against Native Americans, other times against African slaves. But in both cases, the understanding of the difference between those who were "savage" or "heathen" and those who were "Christian" later became the basis upon which American whiteness was built.[2]

---

1. Pedro Font, *Font's Complete Diary of the Second Anza Expedition*, trans. and ed. Hubert Eugène Bolton, vol. 4 of *Anza's California Expeditions* (Berkeley: University of California Press, 1930), 105, quoted in Jonathan Ned Katz, *Gay American History* (New York: Plume, 1992), 291.
2. Jennifer Harvey, *Dear White Christians: For Those Still Longing for Racial Reconciliation* (Grand Rapids: Eerdmans, 2014), 52. According to historian Winthrop D. Jordan (*The White Man's Burden: Historical Origins of Racism in the United States* [London: Oxford University Press, 1974], 52), from the initial contact until the mid-1600s, the terminology the English most often used to describe themselves was "Christian." "Christian" became the identity category distinguishing the English from the "heathen" and "savage" (African and Native peoples). Heathens and savages were considered inferior "others" who might therefore be legitimately treated as such from the perspective of the colonial imperialists making such determinations. From the mid-1600s to 1680, however, Jordan claims that the English began to refer to themselves primarily as "English" and "free." This is notable because during the same period a shift was taking place in the social milieu. At first, though oppression ran rampant, it was so unwieldy and complex that who was master/servant and what kind of labor and economic situation they were in was not entirely predictable based on physical differences. But the lifelong chattel enslavement of people of African descent soon became justified and institutionalized through a variety of legal codes, prolific rhetoric, and powerful ideology. Finally, and most significantly, the unequivocally racial apex of this story came

James Baldwin further articulates the function of this binary when he says, "America became white—the people who, as they claim, 'settled' the country became white—because of the necessity of denying the Black presence and justifying Black subjugation." He goes on to suggest that "no community can be based on such a principle—in other words no community can be established on so genocidal a lie."[3]

It is important to note that these binaries reinforce both one another and the colonizing hierarchies in intersectional ways. For instance, as illustrated above, the very notion of what is savage is predicated upon a violation of the male/female binary. And the corollary is that whatever is civilized vehemently reinforces the male/female binary. Further, these binaries justify the subjugation, torture, exploitation, and genocide of those over whom the colonizer holds power. In fact, much of the genocide of Native peoples throughout the Americas was justified by language around establishing the Holy Faith and the Christian religion, exactly as Pedro Font predicted.

One way in which historical colonization continues in the present-day United States is in the perpetuation of hierarchies that dictate sources of power and sources of vulnerability. Table 1 enumerates some examples.

	Source of Power[4]	Source of Vulnerability
Age	Adult	Child, teenager, or elderly
Race	White	Person of Color
Sex	Male	Female/Intersex
Economic Class	Wealthy	Poor
Education	Holding a degree	Holding no degree
Ability	Physically and mentally able-bodied	Having a mental or physical disability
Sexual Orientation	Heterosexual	Gay, lesbian, or bisexual
Gender Identity	Cisgender	Transgender or genderqueer

at the end of the century. Jordan writes: "after about 1680, taking the colonies as a whole, a new term of self-identification appeared—*white*" (emphasis in the original).

3. James Baldwin, "On Being White and Other Lies," *Essence*, April 1984, 90–92.

Violence and Separation as Tools of Colonization

In order to function, systems of colonization separate people and keep them apart. They seek to squelch the kind of deep, erotic power that is expressed as solidarity, connection, and shared carnal knowledge. Colonizing systems rely upon complicity and silence, and they thrive on the violence of those who possess sources of power acting against those who live primarily in situations of vulnerability.

Historically and in the present-day United States, women and genderqueer people's bodies have been colonized and used as tools of colonization. Those who participated in my research indicated one of the most powerful ways they experienced specific and personal acts of colonization was through the sexual and physical violation of their bodies. Overall, half of the women and genderqueer people surveyed reported sexual and/or physical abuse. For African American respondents, the numbers were more than 75 percent. For those who identified as Hispanic, two-thirds reported abuse. "I have been sexually assaulted two times in my life, at 22 and at 24. Once was a stranger who I offered a ride and once was a man I was dating." "[I experienced] physical, verbal, sexual [abuse]." "I was raped in high school by my best friend's boyfriend." "My first sexual experiences—with a woman and a man—were separate instances of seduction by church leaders. I was also in a marriage in which I was abused, in every way, for seven years." "[I] was molested by my father at 12." "As a child, [I was] sexually and physically abused. Weren't most of us?" Drawing on the power of binaries from above and articulating the ways in which embodiment and sexuality become tools of intersectional colonization, the authors of *Queer (In)justice* state:

> Policing and punishment of sexual and gender "deviance" have existed for centuries in what is now known as the United States. From the first point of contact with European colonizers. . . . Indigenous peoples, enslaved Africans, and immigrants, particularly immigrants of color, were systematically policed and punished based on actual or projected

4. This grid is adapted from Rebecca Voelkel-Haugen and Marie M. Fortune, *Sexual Abuse Prevention: A Course of Study for Teenagers, Revised and Updated* (Cleveland, OH: United Church Press, 1996), 6.

"deviant" sexualities and gender expressions, as an integral part of colonization, genocide and enslavement. . . .

The construction of gender hierarchies and their violent, sexualized enforcement was central to the colonization of this continent. . . . "The colonialism itself, along with the relationships it requires, is inherently raced, gendered, and sexualized."[5]

In order to perpetrate this kind of violence, systems of colonization require the participation of those whose identities fall primarily in "sources of power." Their participation is needed in the actual acts of violence, terror, and abuse, as articulated both in the opening story of the man who stalked the young stripper and in the stories of sexual and physical abuse articulated by others who participated in my research. In the opening story, in the act of scattering the broken glass upon which the young dancer cut her feet, causing her to nearly bleed to death, the stalker accomplished three things. He sought to use violence to reassert his personal power, he utilized violence to reinscribe and metaphorically reinforce the cage of colonization, and he re-created the dominance/submission, male/female binary. Rape and other forms of sexual violence reported above accomplish similar reinforcement of the colonizing system and the power-over dynamic.

The fact that the women and genderqueer people who were also people of color experienced more sexual and physical abuse is an important point to highlight.[6] It is another example of the intersectional power of colonization. The more an individual's identity falls in sources of vulnerability, the more the violence of the colonizing

---

5. Andrea Smith, "Conquest: Sexual Violence and the American Indian Genocide," as quoted in *Queer (In)justice: The Criminalization of LGBT People in the United States*, ed. Joey L. Mogul, Andrea J. Ritchie, and Kay Whitlock (Boston: Beacon Press, 2011), 1f.

6. Movement Advancement Project and Center for American Progress, *Unjust: How the Broken Criminal Justice System Fails Transgender People*, May 2016, PDF, http://tinyurl.com/gvcx5n4, examines how transgender and gender non-conforming people face high levels of discrimination in many areas of life, putting them at risk for economic insecurity, homelessness, and reliance on survival economies. Combined with policing strategies that profile and target transgender people, particularly transgender women of color, the result is high rates of criminalization of transgender people. For example, a shocking 21 percent of transgender women have spent time in prison or jail, compared to only 5 percent of all US adults. And one in five (22 percent) of transgender people report being mistreated by police. Once within the criminal justice system, transgender people are often discriminated against, verbally and sexually assaulted, refused adequate medical care, and treated with utter disregard for their identity and dignity.

system acts to "keep them in their place." This is especially true for transgender women of color without educational or economic resources, who are murdered at very high rates.

Those whose identities are primarily in "sources of power" also participate in colonizing systems through passive nonresistance. Without active resistance to colonizing systems of domination, they become perpetrators of colonization.

First they came for the Socialists, and I did not speak out—

Because I was not a Socialist.
Then they came for the Trade Unionists, and I did not speak out—

Because I was not a Trade Unionist.
Then they came for the Jews, and I did not speak out—

Because I was not a Jew.
Then they came for me—and there was no one left to speak for me.[7]

One cannot help but hear Peter's denial of Jesus in these words from Martin Niemöller, a German pastor who worked in the face of Nazism. He was a white, male, Christian pastor. Without his active resistance to Nazism, he became a perpetrator of it. When he finally chose to stand against Nazism, his previous denial was his undoing because there was no one left to stand for him. Such denial is the lifeblood of colonization. The acts of betrayal and denial are corrosive and further perpetuate the violence of colonization as they inscribe deeper wounds on both the betrayer and betrayed. They further block solidarity and squelch erotic power. Niemöller articulated this well when he wrote:

Thus, whenever I chance to meet a Jew known to me before, then, as a Christian, I cannot but tell him: "Dear Friend, I stand in front of you, but we cannot get together, for there is guilt between us. I have sinned and my people has sinned against thy people and against thyself."[8]

Another way the intersectional violence of colonization functions and

7. Martin Niemöller, *Martin Niemöller: 1892–1984*, ed. James Bentley (New York: Free Press, 1984), 98.
8. Martin Niemöller, *Of Guilt and Hope*, trans. Renee Spodheim (New York: Philosophical Library, 1947), 18.

draws power is through a competition for survival amongst the colonized, which results in horizontal violence as different oppressed groups attack or deny one another. Whether it be the ways in which racism has always been present in efforts to liberate women (in the Women's Suffrage movement, the temperance movement, and the second and third wave feminist movements); the ways in which sexism has functioned within racial justice movements; the ways in which homophobia, biphobia, and transphobia have functioned within women's and racial justice movements; or the ways in which racism and xenophobia have functioned within the LGBTQ movements, horizontal violence has reinforced colonization and served to mitigate solidarity and shared erotic power.

It is important to highlight the ways in which the intersectional violence of colonization works to prevent shared erotic power between different groups of women and genderqueer people. The colonized identity of "womanhood" for white women relies upon the racist binaries of white/heathen, which have become white/black. As bell hooks says, "the socially constructed image of innocent white womanhood relies on the continued production of the racist/sexist sexual myth that black women are not innocent and never can be."[9] These racist binaries result in horizontal violence perpetrated by white women and white genderqueer people against women of color and genderqueer people of color.

Colonizing systems also rely upon the colonized participating in their own degradation through acts of violence directed at the self. Malcolm X describes this violence and the colonization of the mind that led him to do violence when he tells the story of his first "conk."

> This was my first really big step toward self-deprecation: when I endured all of that pain, literally burning my flesh to have it look like a white man's hair. I had joined that multitude of Negro men and women in America who are brainwashed into believing that the black people are "inferior"—and white people are "superior"—they will even violate and mutilate their God-created bodies to try to look "pretty" by white standards.[10]

9. bell hooks, Black Looks: Race and Representation (Boston: South End Press, 1992), 157.
10. Malcolm X, The Autobiography of Malcolm X (New York: Ballantine Books, 1973), 56–57.

Hegemonies

In order to succeed, colonization requires accompanying hegemonies. Hegemony describes at least two different foci: geopolitical and cultural. Geopolitical hegemony is an indirect form of government or imperial dominance in which the *hegemon* (leader state) rules geopolitically subordinate states by the implied means of power, the threat of force, rather than by direct military force. Cultural hegemony, a concept developed by Antonio Gramsci, refers to a context in which one social class can manipulate the system of values and mores of a society in order to create and establish a ruling class, a world view that justifies the status quo of domination of the poor and working classes by the wealthy and ruling classes of the society. Liberation theologians have expanded the concept of cultural hegemony to include world views that justify domination based on race, sex, ability, age, sexual orientation, and gender identity.[11] In contemporary American culture, racism, sexism, homophobia, genderism, ableism, anti-Semitism, Islamophobia, classism, and ageism intertwine and reinforce one another to create a system of interlocking colonizing systems supported by theological hegemonies.

When colonizing hegemonies are directed at those whose identities are primarily in sources of power, an understanding of agency, authority, and rights emerge. The stalker in the opening story believed it was his right to have access to the dancer. When she withheld what was "rightfully his," she was a "cock-teaser" and a "whore." This mindset, which (as we have seen) has been created and supported by theological hegemonies, deludes the colonizer into believing he can own another human being; it perverts the carnal knowledge and sacred connection within God's creation; it crucifies the body of Christ.

These colonizing hegemonies, when directed at those whose identities are in sources of vulnerability and who experience the direct violence of the colonizing system, can be referred to as the

---

11. Antonio Gramsci, *Prison Notebooks*, vol. 1, ed. Joseph A. Buttigieg, trans. Joseph A. Buttigieg and Antonio Callari (New York: Columbia University Press, 1992), 233–38.

colonization of the mind or false consciousness. Parts 3 and 4 will offer examples of colonized peoples resisting colonizing hegemonies and acting in ways to transform systems of colonization. But in this section, it is important to articulate the power of colonizing hegemonies to destroy the colonized.

In this context, the colonized succumb to the power of theological hegemonies. They are unable to choose their own humanity or subjectivity, the carnal knowledge of God, or the erotic power of community. Instead, they directly participate in both physical violence against themselves and adopt the colonizing hegemonies that support such power-over and violence. George Orwell's Winston Smith embodies this false consciousness when he declares: "But it was all right, everything was all right, the struggle was finished. He had won the victory over himself. He loved Big Brother."[12]

This is especially true for people whose bodies are female, of color, old, disabled, queer, or otherwise outside the narrow limits of the hegemonic system. Several survey respondents illustrate the impact of such a context and the power of hegemony to colonize the mind. One woman who identified as African American and biracial articulated, "anyone can 'take' my body away at any time, and I can't protect myself. I learned young to never be caught alone but even that didn't help much." Another, who identified as living with a disability, answered, "I struggle with weight and see myself as ugly and fat through the eyes of others. I hold myself back in the world because I am so ashamed." Another woman who identified as queer answered the question about anything else I should know about her body by responding:

Fatfatfatfatfatfatfatfatfatfatfatfatfatfatfatfatfatfatfatfatfatfatfatfatfat
fatfatfatfatfatfatfatfatfatfatfatfatfatfatfatfatfatfatfatfatfatfatfatfatfat
fatfatfatfatfatfatfatfatfatfatfatfatfatfatfatfatfatfatfatfatfatfatfatfatfat
fatfatfatfatfatfatfatfatfatfatfatfatfatfatfatfatfatfatfatfatfatfatfatfatfat
fatfatfatfatfatfatfatfatfatfatfatfatfatfatfatfatfatfatfatfatfatfatfatfat.[13]

---

12. George Orwell, *1984* (New York: Signet Classics, 1949), 308.
13. This woman filled the entire open-answer box with the word "fat" repeated over and over again. I was moved by the power of her statement about the insidiousness of colonization.

Another example of collective colonization of the mind comes from March of 1969. In that month, *Ebony* magazine was nearly put out of business because they published an issue with a black Jesus on the cover. So many of their subscribers (the vast majority of whom were black) were so upset, they threatened to cancel their subscriptions. The uproar went so far as customers sending in pictures of a white Jesus to replace it.[14] In reaction to this news, Therman Williis writes of the need to decolonize Black consciousness. "Yes, it's like post-slavery syndrome: after 15–20 generations of slavery, and only 5–6 generations post-slavery, how many generations does it take to 'decolonize' to get over the trauma. [The] same can be said about the 15–20 generations of slavemasters, with only 4–5 generations so far, [how many generations does it take] to overcome their trauma of masterhood?"[15]

My own ministry has been filled with pastoring those whose lives have been inexorably marked by the destructive, death-dealing power of theological hegemonies. The story below illustrates my experience with many women, genderqueer, and LGBTQ people with whom I have ministered.

> I was toward the end of my shift at the VA, just checking in on a few last rooms. I didn't know the patient whose door I entered, but as I crossed the threshold and shared that I was the chaplain, I was greeted with a string of expletives whose force was palpable. "Who the [expletive] do you [expletive] think you [expletive] are??" he demanded.
>
> By whatever movement of the Holy Spirit, I chose to stay and bear witness to the anger and pain my metaphorical clerical collar evoked. Somehow I knew I needed to be there.
>
> After he swore at me for several more minutes, he seemed to tire.
>
> Then he asked me what I wanted with him.
>
> I asked if he could tell me a little bit about what made him yell so much at me.

14. Lisa Booker, February 24, 2015, Facebook post, http://tinyurl.com/ht3mjgh.
15. Therman Williis, March 17, 2015, comment on "Yeshua Jah Holiday," Facebook, http://tinyurl.com/hsyyh4n.

What transpired was the beginning of several days of my sitting and listening. He talked of the early years in church when he was told of his sinfulness and worthlessness. He recounted his excommunication when it was learned he was gay. And how his AIDS diagnosis only made it worse. He spoke of simple cruelties and profound ones. In place of care and love, ridicule and revulsion; when he desperately needed tenderness, betrayal came again and again.

And finally, he came to the questions, asked with genuine fear and trembling. "Do you think I'm going to burn in hell? Do you think by this time next week I'll be in the outer darkness?"

As best I could, I tried to speak of love whose strength surpassed even death. I tried to share my heart's conviction that he was a beloved child of God. I attempted to hold a space for love and tenderness to touch his body and soul. . . . And I prayed then and now that somehow, God's fierce tenderness might heal all the pain done in God's name.[16]

---

16. Rebecca Voelkel, "This Complex, Complicated Calling" (sermon, Lyndale United Church of Christ, Minneapolis, August 3, 2014).

4

Sin and Suffering

In the liberation theology tradition, the conversation about sin has been the avenue to name and engage this context of colonization, which separates, dehumanizes, and destroys people and the creation. For liberation theologians, sin is most powerfully observed and known through systems of colonization and oppression—and the hegemonies that support them. This offers a different emphasis and contrasts with other Christian theological traditions, which highlight the individual. In these traditions, it is the individual person acting willfully against God because of weakness or rebellion.[1]

An emphasis on the systemic manifestation of sin parallels part 1's assertion that the incarnation does more than hallow individual bodies/incarnations. The incarnation or Christa/Community blesses the communal relationship and the desire for just and loving relationship among people and peoples. Defining sin as "colonizing systems" recognizes the communal relationship between people and peoples as equally important to the individual. This book, in all four of the "ways" of the matrix, understands that the bodies we are

---

1. Paul R. Sponheim, "Sin and Evil," in *Christian Dogmatics, Vol. 1*, ed. Carl E. Braaten and Robert W. Jenson (Philadelphia: Fortress Press, 1984), 367.

addressing are both the individual person's body and the communal body. Further, just as the individual and communal bodies are blessed, so can individual acts and communal systems be marked by and manifest sin.

A further defining of sin can be found in the young adult novel *A Wind in the Door.* In it, Episcopal novelist, essayist, and theologian Madeleine L'Engle describes God's action in creation as "naming." She writes:

> I fill you with Naming.
> Be!
> Be, butterfly and behemoth,
> be galaxy and grasshopper,
> star and sparrow,
> you matter,
> you are,
> be! . . .
> sing with us,
> dance with us,
> rejoice with us . . .
> Be!
> Sing for the glory
> of the living and the loving
> the flaming of creation
> sing with us
> dance with us
> be with us
> Be![2]

This naming contrasts with L'Engle's image of how sin operates in the world. Sin seeks to un-name, to take away being, to remove significance. This insight is particularly helpful in the context of colonization and adds a needed dimension to our understanding of sin. Sin, then, is as follows: any individual, communal, or systemic state or action that interrupts, breaks, or destroys God's presence in and relationship with and among creation by un-naming, taking away being, or removing the significance of any creature, person, community, or group of people. Such a definition of sin is multifaceted

---

2. Madeleine L'Engle, *A Wind in the Door* (New York: Farrar, Straus & Giroux, 1973), 203–4.

and complex. It is perpetrated on multiple levels. The multifaceted and complex nature of sin is significant given the almost-intractable quality of colonization.

In describing her childhood in Connecticut, Barbara Caruso uses the analogy of snow to describe both the quality of colonization and the ways in which colonization is akin to being caged in sin in ways that seek to destroy freedom of will.

> When I was a little girl I lived in the Connecticut wilderness on a street that turned into a dirt road just a few hundred feet past our house....
>
> Now it snows a lot in Connecticut, and I was not much shorter than I am now. That driveway looked like a glacial cliff. I'd do anything to get out of shoveling it. I'd hem and haw and make excuses.... But it didn't work. The snow would fall. We would shovel. And my parents' response to my whiny "again?" would be an endlessly redundant "yes, again." ... "If it snows," they said, "we shovel"; winter to winter, year to year, we shoveled.
>
> ... When I worked in northern Maine we would notice the first late-September snow because it stuck out after the warmth of summer and the vividness of a short fall. By the middle of the winter, however, we hardly noticed the snow at all. In the northern climes snow is such a daily occurrence that it wasn't until the first-floor windows were completely covered that we became aware the light had gradually been blocked. In fact, the snow distorted the shape and size of everything so much that when it finally melted in the late spring, people would walk around disoriented for a week. You could see where you had been blind before. You could walk on paths that had been snowed over for months. But, in October, November, December, January, February, March, and April, the snow usually fell so quietly that we hardly noticed it. Snow falls so quietly that a person hardly notices it until the door is covered and the smokestack iced over and plugged. It can do this while people sleep. During every Maine winter snow would trap people and asphyxiate them quietly.
>
> ... Together, the snow falling and the snow shoveling represent a lesson my parents taught me. It is this: In order to remove something that is redundant, you must also behave redundantly.
>
> Like snow in the middle of a Maine winter, oppressive structures function by being so normal that they are nearly unseen. We are not talking here about the direct and clear and immediate fear of a tornado, or about outright racist behavior or the supreme misogynist moment when a man

rapes a woman. We are talking about the work of oppression that is a daily redundancy. Slowly it covers the landscape, hiding the black-faced, plaster-cast jockey by the house door. Slowly it blankets the country club golf course that is "restricted." This sort of snow accumulates on top of the history of many peoples, obscuring truth until only a vaguely discernible shadow line indicates where something has been covered.

Gradually it rises to knee-high with explanations like: "We couldn't find anyone" or "He just wasn't right for the job" or with intentional and offensive comments like, "We'll hire one but only if she/he is qualified." Sometimes it's accompanied by accusations that the person who is trying to shovel out "has no sense of humor" or "takes everything too seriously." Eventually, it drifts from one aspect of life to another. It weighs down all possibility of movement. And then, finally it blocks the door and fills the stack. And in the night, the unnoticed weight of oppression kills. Like snow in winter months in the north of this country, the daily redundancy of oppression kills.[3]

The Crucifixion and Resurrection

In part 1, I suggested that womanist theologian Delores Williams's understanding of the "solidarity of the cross" was key to understanding the incarnation. The crucifixion is also critically important as we engage the sin of colonization. This assertion arises from many places, including my own lived experience.

In 1987, I was part of a delegation that spent a week in Santa Marta, El Salvador. We were part of the Accompaniment Movement, which sought to have a religious presence to protest the death squads and violence of the US-backed Salvadoran government. One of the most important moments of that trip, one that marked my coming to an adult faith, occurred when I met a woman who was a "delegate of the Word." These Bible-study leaders were often the ones the death squads targeted in order to terrorize an entire community. While describing her work, she shared that she had lost five children to the civil war, one of whom she had seen tortured to death. When I asked her how it was that she had survived, she said:

3. Barbara Caruso, "On Being Redundant: Freedom Is Not Once" (baccalaureate address, Earlham College, Richmond, IN, June 9, 1991). Used by permission.

I have been able to survive because I know that in Jesus Christ, God knows in His body what it means to be tortured to death. So my son did not die alone, but being held in God's arms. And in the resurrection, God has said, once and for all, that life and love are stronger than death. So, it doesn't matter what they try to do to me. Even if they kill me, I know that God will resurrect me. And that makes me powerful.[4]

This understanding that the crucifixion of Jesus is an act of God's radical solidarity with the victims of colonization is critically important to the *Via Negativa*. It places God squarely with the oppressed and powerfully for the marginalized. It highlights that the cross represents another aspect of God's carnal knowledge.

In the crucifixion, God knows through the bodily experience of Jesus what it means to be tortured to death by the empire's representatives. Roman soldiers (the representatives of the colonizing empire) seek to un-name Jesus. He is tortured and hung on a cross outside the city/body politic with criminals. Empire makes a travesty of his messianic mission. His body is violated—he is beaten, mocked, and sexually abused as people poke at his genitals. This bodily violation, this torture, this sexual abuse is what happens to the colonized every day. In the crucifixion, God has firsthand empathy and embodied solidarity with the reality of this omnipresent suffering in people's lives, particularly the suffering that is caused by colonization and the present-day representatives of empire.[5]

There is deeper and more revolutionary meaning in the crucifixion and resurrection, however. Not only is God-in-Jesus radically present in resisting the colonizing systems and hegemonies that seek to crucify love and justice, but God-in-Jesus hallows that which seeks to restore, heal, and transform suffering. The resurrection suggests that healing our bodies, claiming the blessing and pleasure they can offer, and delighting in our embodiment are all ways in which we can stand in solidarity with God's intention in creation. This resistance, healing, and pleasure will be explored in more depth in part 3.

---

4. Co-Madre of the Mothers of the Disappeared, interview by author, San Salvador, El Salvador, December 28, 1987.
5. Matthew Fox, "Moving Beyond a Cross Fetish: The Empty Tomb and Creation Spirituality," *Tikkun*, October 28, 2012, http://tinyurl.com/jfmlcx2.

Desire, Longing, and Pleasure Distorted

When sin as colonization and its supporting theological hegemonies are present, desire, longing, and pleasure are distorted. As I explored in part 1, it is our longing for connection, justice, and love that is part of God's good gift of embodiment and sexuality. Our desires are one way in which God communicates God's intentions both for relationship with us and for our relationships with one another. Implicit in such longing and desire is the full humanity and subjectivity of another person or community of people. Inherent in such longing and desire is the requirement of just and loving communities and systems.

When the humanity and subjectivity of the other person or people are held in the context of just and loving communities, then desire, longing, and pleasure are marked by erotic, sacred power. What draws us toward one another is a longing for the embodied, justice-filled, loving purpose of deeper connection and shared carnal knowledge and power with God. Particularly when desire, longing, and pleasure arise out of those who have been the victims of colonization, they function as profound resistance to hegemony.

However, in the context of colonization, where power is marked by domination, exploitation, and objectification, the erotic powers of longing, desire, and pleasure are distorted and used as tools of harm. Instead of building connection between people who are seen as full subjects and beloved children of God, they are used as weapons to break connection, dehumanize the object, and desecrate God's creation. As such, the erotic powers of longing, desire, and pleasure become the pornographic powers of addiction,[6] coveting, and

---

6. I recognize that using the language of "pornographic" and "erotic" is controversial, but I first both learned and helped to develop this analysis during the World Council of Churches United States Urban-Rural Mission sponsored Sexuality and Community gatherings that took place from 1999 to 2001. The gathering brought together thirty people for reflection and thought-partnership around the subject of sexuality and community. The group consisted of twenty-five people of color from First Nations, Latinx, African American, and Asian American Pacific Islander communities and five white people from a variety of ethnic backgrounds. Half of us were based in Christian communities and half were community activists. Half were LGBTQI and half identified as straight. In this context, we grappled with how to language a colonized sexuality/embodiment and differentiate it from a liberated or non-colonized sexuality/embodiment. The contrast between erotic and pornographic was our best attempt.

disembodied gratification. Any exploration of the *Via Negativa* must take seriously this pornographic distortion and destruction.

The opening story of part 2 offers a poignant and profound example of the pornographic distortion of desire, longing, and pleasure. The stalker regarded the dancer not as a fellow human being, subject of her own life and beloved child of God, but rather as an object that was his to possess for a few twenty-dollar bills. He coveted her; he sought her to gratify him. He wanted to dominate, possess, and subjugate her.

There is another way that desire, longing, and pleasure become distorted into addiction. When those who are entangled in colonization—either as oppressors or oppressed—experience a fissure in the hegemony that supports colonization, they have a choice to make. They can use that fissure as an opportunity for solidarity, resistance, or liberation. When this happens, life-giving, erotic power is released. But sometimes those caged in colonization encounter a metaphorical loose bar or realize that someone else has successfully sawn through the bars of the cage, and they choose to turn their backs or seek a means to refocus on the reality of the cage. In order to accomplish this, they need help. They need something to crush erotic connection. They need something to redirect their passion. This soul-crushing, passion-killing tool often comes through addiction to drugs or alcohol. A powerful example of this comes from the Civil War period in the United States.

Mary Boykin Chesnut was married to a man who served in Confederate President Jefferson Davis's cabinet, and she was a passionate supporter of the Confederate cause. In her diaries, however, she articulates the psychological and spiritual impact of slavery on her. Much like Niemöller's confession, her testimony dramatically illustrates that colonization has soul-crushing implications for all—including those whose identities are primarily in sources of power. Upon witnessing a slave auction, she reports the "tragedy" she observed.

> A mad woman taken from her husband and children. Of course she was mad, or she would not have given her grief words in that public place.

Her keepers were along. What she said was rational enough, pathetic at times, at times heart-rending. It excited me so I quietly took opium. It enabled me to retain every particle of mind or sense or brains I have, so quiets my nerves that I can calmly reason and take rational views of things otherwise maddening.[7]

In the midst of the brutality of colonization that chattel slavery in the United States was, Chesnut chose not to respond with empathy for the woman who was being torn from her husband and children. Chesnut clearly understood and felt the horror of bearing witness to such agony, calling it "heart-rending." But she chose the oppressor's route of passive nonresistance and paid the price. She had to practice addiction, using opium to crush her empathy and her passion for connection, and "calming" her in ways that restored "reason" and "rational views."

Mortality and Physical Disabilities

Another facet of embodiment and sexuality in the *Via Negativa* is the fragility of bodies. Aging bodies, death, separation, bodies in pain, and disability are all realities whose presence cannot be ignored. Even outside the context of colonization, bodies die, menopause happens, illness occurs. Embodiment is a locus of suffering. Many of the survey respondents illustrate this point. "I was in an accident 34 years ago, and the injuries I sustained have had a lasting impact on my life." "[I live with] fibromialgia [sic] [and] arthritis." "I have RA." "I have depression, asthma, high blood pressure, and sleep disorders. All 'hidden' but all affect my identity and abilities and my quality of life." "[I'm] getting creakier as I age."[8] One woman articulated it this way:

[I struggled with my body] being weaker and slower than most boys and men; being an automatic victim b/c cannot adequately defend self; being taught to tilt my head and smile and flirt to get my needs met, instead of just asking straight on for help like a guy would, or being taught how to do it myself; being told my knees looked fat; wearing glasses since childhood

---

7. Mary Boykin Chesnut in Mab Segrest, *Born to Belonging: Writings on Spirit and Justice* (New Brunswick, NJ: Rutgers University Press, 2002), 140.
8. Voelkel, "Women, Our Bodies and Spirit."

and looking like a nerd or geek instead of a sex symbol in junior high and high school; being afraid of the ball and of physical contact and of letting people down, thus avoiding team sports; being expected to cheer on other athletes instead of being an athlete myself; being expected to be a jock b/c my dad was and my brother was; feeling less than all the other girls, except those who were clearly less attractive than [I] was, and feeling guilty for noticing and caring.[9]

As this woman illustrates, suffering or disability in the context of colonization can, at times, become exponentially more difficult and even torturous. One survey respondent spoke about the ways unjust economic systems complicate her pain: "I sustained a work-related injury almost four years ago that has exacerbated into a condition involving both knees and my lumbar region. The pain is constant and intractable, I have no insurance, and a former employer who is fighting me at every turn. I look fine, but I am severely limited in my physical activities and endurance."[10] Another respondent used almost mundane language to describe the manifestation of colonization in her life: "[I live with] chronic pain in my hands, arms, shoulders due to police brutality. [It's] not limiting necessarily but fatiguing."[11] Another respondent suggested pain and suffering that had chiseled themselves into her life when she answered simply, "PTSD."[12]

While the context of colonization, sin, crucifixion, and suffering is a contemporary reality in the United States, it is not an ultimate one. We move now to the next part of the matrix, the *Via Creativa*. It is there that we encounter the truth that, while sin and death are powerful and must be engaged, we need other parts of the matrix as well to speak of all that God is doing.

9. Ibid.
10. Ibid.
11. Ibid.
12. Ibid.

PART III

Via Creativa—The Creative Way

The *Via Creativa* is the part of the theological matrix in which creativity, procreativity, resistance, and resurrection live. It is marked by joy, resurrection, dance, music, and the artistic impulse to liberate and transform. The *Via Creativa* is not afraid of the *Via Negativa*; instead, it offers laughter and tears, courage and creation to transform systems of colonization and sin.

But the *Via Creativa* is not naïve or rooted in false consciousness. It knows that when a person or community is colonized, un-named, and terrorized, fear and despair are often the only responses. Not every person or every community can resist or practice resurrection. The *Via Creativa* asserts that in the face of the destructive power of colonization, it becomes the vocation of those who can witness to hope. On behalf of those whom colonization has successfully un-named or broken, the resistors practice resurrection. The resistors embody the reality that life, love, and justice are more powerful than death.

In his masterpiece about the Holocaust, Elie Wiesel tells the story of one such man, Juliek, who carries his violin with him as he is being transported to Buchenwald.[1] He refuses to give up his humanity and

---

1. I want to be careful in using this example that I am not co-opting Jewish experience. I am not suggesting that Juliek or Wiesel practice resurrection, which is a profoundly Christian understanding and one that has been used to perpetrate brutality against Jews. Instead, I hope

gives a concert of Beethoven as a reminder that all his fellow prisoners are human, too.

> I heard the sound of the violin. The sound of a violin, in this dark shed. . . . What madman could be playing the violin here, at the brink of his own grave? . . .

> It must have been Juliek.

> He played a fragment from Beethoven's concerto. I had never heard sounds so pure. In such a silence. . . .

> It was pitch dark. I could hear only the violin, and it was as though Juliek's soul were the bow. He was playing his life. The whole of his life was gliding on the strings—his last hopes, his charred past, his extinguished future. He played as he would never play again.[2]

Wiesel's story illustrates the revolutionary power of resistance and the ways in which Jewish practices of justice and claiming life can help illuminate the Christian theological project I am about.

2. Elie Wiesel, *Night* (New York: Bantam Books, 1982), 90.

5

Alternatives to Despair

Resistance and Resurrection

In response to the devastation of colonization and its accompanying theological hegemonies, there exists a power that resists. In that resistance resides creativity, laughter, joy, and passion. These are some of the most powerful tools of decolonization and liberation.

There is no more poignant and precise Christian claim than resurrection to resist colonization, destruction, and death and embody decolonization and liberation. In the biblical narrative, Jesus is executed by means reserved for Roman political prisoners, crucifixion, rather than by means used for violators of Jewish law, namely stoning.[1] His crucifixion is an act of solidarity with all those whose lives have been taken by the hands of unjust political systems and the hegemonies that justify them. God's resurrection of Jesus is a direct response to the crucifixion. Though colonization, destruction, and death may have scored a momentary victory, the resurrection announces that justice, life, and God's power not only resist such

---

1. The crucifixion is present in all four canonical gospels: Matt 27:33–44, Mark 15:22–32, Luke 23:33–43, and John 19:17–25.

momentary success but claim ultimate reality. It is not a coincidence that the story of Jesus's crucifixion and resurrection is known as "the passion."[2]

In her masterpiece, *They Have Threatened Us with Resurrection*, Guatemalan poet Julia Esquivel articulates this resurrection reality and illustrates how it becomes a strategy for resistance. She speaks of those who have suffered and died, and, powerfully, turns Good Friday into Easter with her startling notion that those dead are threatening us with resurrection, which the powers-that-be will not be able to stop:

> They have threatened us with Resurrection
> because they will not be able to take away from us
> their bodies,
> their souls,
> their strength,
> their spirit,
> not even their death
> and least of all their life. . . .
>
> They have threatened us with Resurrection,
> because they are more alive than ever before,
> because they transform our agonies
> and fertilize our struggle,
> because they pick us up when we fall. . . .
>
> That is the whirlwind
> which does not let us sleep,
> the reason why sleeping, we keep watch,
> and awake, we dream. . . .
>
> Join us in this vigil
> and you will know what it is to dream!
> Then you will know how marvelous it is
> To live threatened with Resurrection!
>
> To dream awake,
> to keep watch asleep,
> to live while dying,
> and to know ourselves already
> resurrected![3]

2. The Gospel passion narratives are a "double header," featuring the strenuous passion of crucifixion and the even more forceful passion of resurrection.

Knowing ourselves "already resurrected" is a passion story, too. Claiming resurrection in our own lives creates energy, passion, and joy. These manifest in courage and stamina, which resist the power of colonization. In her novel about female genital mutilation, *Possessing the Secret of Joy*, Alice Walker examines the themes of colonization and resistance. She concludes her book with this passage, as the protagonist is being led to her execution for killing the woman whose role it had been to perform hers and the community's female genital mutilations:

> THE WOMEN ALONG the way have been warned they must not sing. Rockjawed men with machine guns stand facing them. But women will be women. Each woman standing beside the path holds a red-beribboned, closely swaddled baby in her arms, and as I pass, the bottom wrappings fall. The women then place the babies on their shoulders or on their heads, where they kick their naked legs, smile with pleasure, screech with terror, or occasionally wave. It is a protest and celebration the men threatening them do not even recognize. At the moment of crisis I realize that, because my hands are bound, I cannot adjust my glasses, and therefore must tilt my head awkwardly in order to locate and focus on a blue hill. It is while I am distracted by this maneuver that I notice there is a blue hill rising above and just behind the women and their naked-bottomed little girls, who now stand in rows fifty feet in front of me. In front of them kneels my little band of intent faces. Mbati is unfurling a banner, quickly, before the soldiers can stop her. . . . All of them—Adam, Olivia, Benny, Pierre, Raye, Mbati—hold it firmly and stretch it wide.
>
> RESISTANCE IS THE SECRET OF JOY! it says in huge block letters. There is a roar as if the world cracked open and I flew inside. I am no more. And satisfied.[4]

There is an interrelating, interpenetrating, mutually expounding relationship amongst resistance, creativity, laughter, joy, and passion. Resistance both fuels and is fueled by creativity, laughter, joy, and passion. All of these reside within the individual's body and the body of the community.

3. Julia Esquivel, "They Have Threatened Us with Resurrection," in *Threatened with Resurrection: Prayers and Poems from an Exiled Guatemalan* (Elgin, IL: Brethren Press, 1994), 61–65. Permission obtained from Brethren Press editor, James Steetan, February 11, 2013, for use in this work.
4. Alice Walker, *Possessing the Secret of Joy* (New York: Harcourt, Brace, Jovanovich, 1992), 270–80.

It is important to note that anger can also be a powerful fuel for resistance. Anger can be the force that cracks the grip of false consciousness; it can be the way out of depression. Channeled anger can be a way of asserting dignity and humanity. Anger can be one way to keep one's name. One cannot help but imagine that it was anger that propelled Sojourner Truth to respond with her "Ain't I a Woman" speech in the face of un-naming.[5] Surely it was anger that fueled Fannie Lou Hamer's televised testimony before the 1964 Credentials Committee of the Democratic National Convention in Atlantic City, in which she declared, "I am sick and tired of being sick and tired" and described in detail her experience of being beaten for her Civil Rights work, all of which proved to be a pivotal shift in the movement.[6]

It is also important to note that unchanneled anger can become corrosive, embittering, and death-dealing, especially if it is a long-term strategy. As the primary tool of resistance, anger can become perverted and distorted, and, painfully, inscribe relationships based in hatred, violence, and un-naming. Examples of this perversion are far too prevalent, including battered women who batter their children and revolutionaries who, once they have overthrown a dictatorship, establish oppressive regimes. Jesus named this kind of corrosive anger when he told the parable of the unforgiving servant who, though his debts were cancelled, turned around and reinscribed relationships of power-over with those who owed him money (Matt 18:21–35).

In my estimation, it is not coincidental that the best illustrations of resistance and resurrection as part of the *Via Creativa* come through artistic expression. As evidenced in part 1, the artistic impulse is directly connected to the divine gift of embodiment. Love, passion, and creativity are created as mutually referent gifts. Therefore, the role of the artist in the liberative practice of resistance and resurrection is critically important. The artistic impulse within both the person and the community is one way the *Via Creativa* manifests itself. Writer

5. Corona Brezina, *Sojourner Truth's "Ain't I a Woman?" Speech: A Primary Source Investigation* (New York: RosenCentral Primary Source, 2005).
6. Lottie L. Joiner, "Remembering Civil Rights Heroine Fannie Lou Hamer: 'I'm Sick and Tired of Being Sick and Tired,'" *The Daily Beast*, September 2, 2014, http://tinyurl.com/hbv342n.

James Baldwin speaks to this reality, "The role of the artist is exactly the same as the role of the lover. If I love you, I have to make you conscious of the things you don't see."[7]

There is a connection, then, between the artistic impulse and concrete acts of resistance to colonization. One way to describe this connection comes from the Center for Artistic Activism. They talk about "ethical spectacles," which are actions that "ravishingly illuminate and dramatize real-world power dynamics and social relations that otherwise tend to remain hidden in plain sight."[8] Ethical spectacles explicitly link artists and activists; they challenge those who resist colonization to develop aesthetic strategies for rediscovering erotic justice and claiming liberation.

Two examples of ethical spectacles help articulate just how much power is released when art and activism are interwoven.

[The film] *Selma* is the story of a group of people collectively creating and performing the most powerful "ethical spectacle" they can think of in order to move American hearts and minds to support Civil Rights. . . . These activists did not go to art school, yet the devastating images of their protests in Selma that tore through mainstream media—the peaceful marchers brutalized by police on horseback during the first march across the Edmund Pettis Bridge and the determined multitude that returned to march again—were the direct outcome of the organizers' aesthetic strategy. . . . And it worked.

. . . [The film] *Larry Kramer: In Love and Anger* is a study in "ethical spectacle." Kramer is an artist whose outrage incited AIDS activism in this country in the 1980s, humanized the way the medical industrial complex treats suffering people in clinical drug trials, and expedited the discovery of the medication that saved Kramer's life and the lives of millions around the globe who are now living with AIDS. In the film, Dr. Tony Fauci, Director of the National Institute for Allergies and Infectious Diseases since AIDS first became part of our public consciousness, states: "There's medicine before Larry Kramer and medicine after Larry Kramer."

What Kramer and a host of artists and activists in New York (including

---

7. James Baldwin, "The Black Scholar Interviews James Baldwin," in *Conversations with James Baldwin*, ed. Fred L. Standley and Louis H. Pratt (Jackson: University Press of Mississippi, 1989), 156.

8. Stephen Duncombe, *Dream: Re-Imagining Progressive Politics in an Age of Fantasy* (New York: New Press, 2007), 126.

myself) did was take art and theater into the streets. From putting a rather large condom on the home of the notoriously anti-gay, anti-sex-education North Carolina Senator Jesse Helms to throwing ashes of our loved ones onto the White House lawn, we expressed our outrage in ways that the news and the public could not ignore.[9]

In both of these examples, artistic expression exposes the fact that systems of colonization and the hegemonies that support them tell lies both about those who are oppressed and about the oppressors. When art and activism are intertwined, they become resistance in four ways.

First, they help people see what we previously did not see or, perhaps more accurately, refused to see. The violence present at Selma was nothing new. It was centuries old. But through the work of both the activists/artists who planned the march and, later, the activists/artists who made the film, which attracted *New York Times* and other journalists, the scales fell from the eyes of the oppressors.

Second, when art and activism are intertwined, they embody and assert a reclamation of God as lover—and a hallowing of the bodies with whom God has carnal knowledge. Larry Kramer, Macky Alston, and the other artists/activists were claiming the beauty and power of those who had died of AIDS. They were claiming that their bodies had been an incarnation. They were naming them beloved in the sight of God. Third, the intertwining of art and activism can make the future goal real in the present in sacramental ways. Juliek's violin playing broke, if only momentarily, the colonizer's grip. Juliek named himself and all who heard him when he played Beethoven. Fourth, the artistic/activist connection becomes resistance because it can link past and future resistance.

I will develop in more detail the ways in which the third and fourth elements of the artistic/activist connection become resistance in part 4's exploration of the *Via Transformativa*. But here it is important to name explicitly the role of time in the activist/artist aesthetic strategy. Part of the artistic endeavor, for the individual or the community, can be the experience of "losing track of time" or being "in

9. Macky Alston, "The Power and Pleasure You Can Unleash When Your Inner Artist Joins Your Inner Activist," *Huffington Post*, February 17, 2015, http://tinyurl.com/zrv32fr.

the zone." Artistic expression can give the artist or artistic community a momentary (or longer) experience of being transported out of the conditions of colonization and oppression. One example of this is the experiences of American, Australian, and British women who were interned in a Japanese camp during World War Two. They turned to music to face into the conditions of captivity and violence.

> They had nothing but suffering, these women, held captive in a Japanese prison camp in Southeast Asia during World War II. They were separated from their parents and husbands, abused by brutal guards, starving, filthy, diseased, with no end to their misery in sight.
>
> But on Christmas 1943, they had music.
>
> Thanks to two prisoners—one a society matron who had been trained at London's Royal Academy of Music, the other a Presbyterian missionary—they had Dvorak, they had Mendelssohn, they had Chopin, Debussy, Brahms. Norah Chambers, the musician, and Margaret Dryburgh, the missionary, transcribed the pieces from memory and taught a choir of English, Dutch and Australian women prisoners to sing the instrumental parts. . . .
>
> The music conveyed beauty, dignity and order in a world of ugliness, ignominy and chaos. Decades later, camp inmate and vocal orchestra member Betty Jeffrey wrote . . . from her home in Australia to say, "When I sang that vocal orchestra music, I forgot I was in the camp. I felt free."[10]

This experience of freedom—transported out of time, out of the external conditions of colonization or bondage for a moment—is one of the ways the *Via Creativa* fosters resistance and resurrection. If only momentarily, colonization is defeated. The future goal becomes present as the un-naming sought by the colonizer becomes the collective act of naming and claiming of personhood and humanity.

Binary Busting

One embodied strategy for resistance that both employs an aesthetic strategy and emerges from genderqueer and intersectional wisdom is

---

10. Rod Dreher, "'Paradise Road' Camp Prisoners Recall the Music of Survival," *Lubbock Avalanche-Journal*, April 24, 1997.

that of challenging hegemonic binaries like male/female, dominance/submission, white/black, heathen/Christian. Gloria Anzaldúa spoke of being asked to choose between being Chicana and lesbian. The image she used was that of a line in the sand in which Chicana and lesbian were two separate nations on either side of the border and each nation demanded her loyalty. But instead of choosing to live in one or the other, she employed a both/and strategy in which she metaphorically created a borderland that was Chicana lesbian.[11] This both/and way of being busts open colonization's insistence on either/or binaries and utilizes intersectionality's multiplicities to claim a continuum of identity rather than two opposing points. This binary busting is a very queer practice. This is highlighted in a comment by one respondent to the survey.

> I take pride in the fact that people cannot place me in the same category from one day to the next. Society generally wants to categorize me as a Lesbian. I am flattered by this, because the term is a powerful statement against patriarchy. I use it to describe myself when I want to use its powerful connotations. However, my sexuality is a bit more expansive than that term connotes. But, most people don't know how to deal with the identity of queer.[12]

Procreation

There exists a deep connection between the lover, the artist, and the activist. The desire and passion to create—art, sculpture, beauty—is intimately connected to the desire and longing to make love and make justice in the world.[13] This is true for the creators of ethical spectacles and it is true for the likes of Emma Goldman who famously declared, "If I can't dance, I don't want to be part of your revolution."[14]

---

11. Gloria Anzaldúa, *Borderlands/La Frontera: The New Mestiza*, 4th ed. (San Francisco: Aunt Lute Books, 2012).
12. Voelkel, "Women, Our Bodies and Spirit."
13. Heyward, "Sexuality, Love, and Justice," 295.
14. Emma Goldman paraphrased from *Living My Life* (New York: Dover Publications, 1970), 56. It has been claimed that Emma Goldman never literally spoke those famous words. In her autobiography, *Living My Life* (1931), she describes how she was once admonished for dancing at a party in New York and was told "that it did not behoove an agitator to dance. Certainly not with such reckless abandon, anyway." Goldman responded furiously: "I did not believe that a Cause which stood for a beautiful ideal, for anarchism, for release and freedom from conventions and

These same desires and passions can be connected to the desire to birth children. Many women with whom I have spoken have noted the parallels between gestating a child and gestating an idea, a project, or a piece of beauty or art. Joy, passion, and desire connect to giving birth—to ideas, to justice, to children. One woman in the survey noted:

> I have four healthy children all of whom I have breastfed until age two or three. I am astoundingly proud that my body conceived them, gestated them, birthed them and nourished them. Even given that profound appreciation I have body issues. I am overweight and I am working on loving my body in spite of that. Never the less [sic], my relationship with God/ess has grown directly because of my feelings about my experience with my own body and the birth experience. I am truly in awe which has led to a closer experience with the divine.[15]

Through the experience of gestating, birthing, and nourishing a child, this woman (and many other respondents to my survey) identified with God and connected to God's passion. Just as God has carnal knowledge of creation—God is deeply rooted in it and is the root of all desire for goodness and justice—many of the women who gave birth articulated similar bonds with their children. This co-creative energy and embodied connection to God's passion can be another crucial strategy in resisting the death-dealing, un-naming work of colonization.

It is important to note, however, that the resistance is not ever complete. Even as this woman was able to experience co-creativity with God, she was not completely freed to love her own body. The power of colonization continued to dwell within her "body issues." This is why resistance against colonization, rather than its defeat, is one of the strategies of the *Via Creativa*.

---

prejudice, should demand the denial of life and joy. I insisted that our Cause could not expect me to become a nun and that the movement should not be turned into a cloister. If it meant that, I did not want it." This episode was later paraphrased and transformed into the famous quote.

15. Voelkel, "Women, Our Bodies and Spirit."

6

———

Embodied Practices of Hope

Expansive Passion

One of the ways in which the *Via Creativa* operates is the multiplying effect of creativity. Several of the survey respondents noted that creativity, laughter, joy, and passion have an expansive quality to them. That is to say, the energy and passion of love for another person is connected to love of their life circumstances and these are connected to a deep desire to make this kind of love, justice, and joy in the world. To paraphrase several of the respondents, joy and passion are deeply personal, but they repeatedly lead to passion, love, and justice in the community and in the world.[1]

In many ways, this is the heart of solidarity. It is what empowered Archbishop Óscar Romero to undergo the transformation that took him from a conservative defender of the institutional Catholic Church and the repressive Salvadoran government to a fiery, fearless proponent of justice. Before the March 12, 1977, assassination of Father Rutilio Grande, Romero's appointment to the archbishop role was

1. Voelkel, "Women, Our Bodies and Spirit."

welcomed by government officials and bemoaned by liberation theologians. But when Grande, a close personal friend, was gunned down for his work serving and helping the poor, Romero's love for him expanded to include those whom Grande loved. "When I looked at Rutilio lying there dead I thought, 'If they have killed him for doing what he did, then I too have to walk the same path.'"[2]

Sport and Dance

Romero's transformation included a shift in how he understood the bodies of poor people. Submitting to the expansive quality of passion allowed him to move from understanding poor bodies as expendable to understanding those bodies as incarnational, as embodiments of the divine. This same shift is critical for those whose bodies have been colonized. Hallowing one's own colonized body is a critical part of resistance and resurrection.

Several people who participated in the survey spoke of finding liberation in moving their bodies in dance and sport. The act of claiming the beauty and power of their bodies challenged the colonization of female and genderqueer bodies and affirmed the *Via Creativa*.[3] Here are a few examples of respondents reflecting on sport and movement:

> Dancing hula and other forms of dance have been very important to developing a positive body image. Participating in sports has also been important in that same way. Our culture places so much emphasis on how female bodies look. I enjoy activities that help me feel my body, and work to improve what I can do.[4]

2. Michael A. Hayes and David Tombs, *Truth and Memory: The Church and Human Rights in El Salvador and Guatemala* (Leominster, UK: Gracewing Publishing, 2001), 48.
3. It is particularly interesting that 2012 marked the fortieth anniversary of Title IX, which reads, "no person in the United States shall, on the basis of sex, be excluded from participation in, be denied the benefits of, or be subjected to discrimination under any education program or activity receiving federal financial assistance." Title IX revolutionized the participation of girls and women in sports as well as a myriad of areas of study such as medicine, the law, and the sciences. This illustrates the power of colonization and the connections between legal code, theological hegemonies, and cultural practices in either oppressing people or contributing to their liberation. For more information about Title IX and its impact on women in sport, see the Title IX Blog, http://title-ix.blogspot.com/.
4. Voelkel, "Women, Our Bodies and Spirit."

Sports taught me that I was in charge of my body and that I could control, change and utilize it.[5]

I love being an athlete and being healthy to support my athletics. I love rugby because all shapes and sizes are welcomed and big is good![6]

My body and I have not always been friends. I used to hate the way I looked. I was bulimic for a short time. Believe it or not, what helped me to stop (besides my honesty about it among my besties) was stripping. I became a stripper as a freshman in college. Before dancing, I had a difficult time standing up to people, when they'd insult or criticize me. At the club, my dancer persona was strong, sassy, sexy, and confident. She didn't need anyone's approval. When I realized that her persona was a part of me, I absorbed those qualities into myself. I still struggle with body image issues, but they are not as extreme as they used to be. Bodies are beautiful.[7]

I hid my body for a long time—baggy clothes, etc. I'm feminine, fairly thin, got a lot of notice (and still do) for how I look, especially from men, which made me uncomfortable. About 10 years ago I started bellydance classes and found a way to think of being feminine as a strength, not a weakness that could be exploited. Now I feel strong and feminine and not concerned if people look at me and find me attractive, because I don't fear them/ don't feel weak now.[8]

Empowered Sex and Creative Sexual Theology

Another area that flows out of this understanding of feeling "in one's body" is that of empowered sex. Survey respondents reported that empowered sex was critically important to them. In the face of bodily violations based on ability, race, gender identity, sex, sexual orientation, age, and a myriad of other forms of colonizing violence, respondents remarked on the importance of empowerment and self-determination in sexual practice. In order to resist colonization, sex became, for some, an arena for creativity, passion, joy, and play. For some, their sexual practice was empowered and self-determined precisely because it did not conform to the standards set by colonizing

5. Ibid.
6. Ibid.
7. Ibid.
8. Ibid.

hegemonies; for others, there was experimentation with many practices followed by a more established pattern. The following three quotes illustrate the wide range and possibly contradictory understandings survey respondents showed when asked to describe their creative, empowered sexual expressions:

> I have a lot of sex. I'm non-monogamous with three partners of three different religious persuasions (liturgical ecumenical Christian, non-theistic Quaker, and pagan UU [Unitarian Universalist]). I masturbate when I want, have partnered sex frequently, and have active BDSM relationships with all three partners.[9]

> I'm chuckling now because over my many years I've experimented with every choice you offered [in the survey question]. What I learned for me was that I am most comfortable being in a relationship with only one person. I found S&M [sadomasochism] to be very intense, but totally lacking in that whole concept of unconditional acceptance between two people, and the relationship is a huge part of the entire package for me. I haven't felt any need or desire to masturbate for many years now. We don't use toys because Nature gave us all the tools we need. I think for both of us "keeping it real" is important, and fantasy games just aren't a part of our lives. Just sharing and being able to make happy the woman I love is sufficient.[10]

> I get really mad at my partner sometimes because we have very different styles or ways of expressing our selves. And then we go to bed and I am reminded of this special amazing dance we do together that is so good and loving and hot and it seals me back into the commitment I have made to be with him. It's an affirmation of who we are together.—I love that I have had a very open and satisfying sex life. It just makes me so confident and brings me great joy. In spite of the harm I have survived.—The humor, the play, the way that sex and sexuality augment our lives on this earth.—polyamory for me is an expression of freedom. It's very important to me that my body is not anyone's possession. Even if we only play 1 or 2 times a year—the fact that there's "no lock on the door" makes me very very happy.[11]

It is important to acknowledge that, even for those who intentionally

---

9. Voelkel, "Women, Our Bodies and Spirit." BDSM is a variety of erotic practices or roleplaying involving bondage, dominance, and submission, and sadomasochism.
10. Ibid.
11. Ibid.

seek to practice empowered sex, sex is sometimes boring. Other times, even as a strategy of resistance, sex can be practiced in such a way as to reinscribe colonization in destructive ways. Such is the reach and breadth of colonized sexuality. But I would argue, particularly in the context of the *Via Creativa*, that S&M and BDSM practices are not, in and of themselves, reinscribing colonization. As I spoke with women and genderqueer people who practiced S&M and BDSM, as illustrated by the quote above, they spoke of their practice as performance, almost in the same sense as ethical spectacle. Both parties were explicit about the power they were both playing with and caricaturing. Many of them were literally role-playing in ways that sought to expose and comment upon power.

S&M and BDSM practices are not liberating strategies for everyone. In fact, the majority of women and genderqueer people with whom I spoke did not think they would be liberating. But an important part of this book and of this matrix is that multiplicity, particularity, and context are to be valued and recognized. No one pattern of sexual practice is life-giving. What is empowering for some, given their experience and context, may be disempowering for others. What is liberative in one context may prove oppressive in another.

For the purposes of the *Via Creativa*, I find the above responses particularly interesting and helpful. Each person has engaged the questions of what s/he wants sexually and what the role of power and ownership are to be in hir sexual expressions.[12] Out of engaging these issues, s/he has chosen a path of creativity and play. Such a process of empowerment, self-reflection, and agency in the context of a colonization that seeks to mitigate against these is evidence of decolonization and liberation. In other words, empowered sex that combines self-determination, negotiation, and experimentation can be one way to practice being where one wants to be in the present moment. This is a powerful way of embodying the future vision now. Additionally, those who participate in unconventional sexual practices

---

12. For a definition and explanation of the usage of s/he and hir, see the glossary section marked Gender Pronouns.

can anticipate a transformed and liberated world order when they do so in ways that are rooted in shared erotic power.

Creative Sexual Theology

Because women's and genderqueer people's bodies are sites of colonizing violence, particularly sexual violence, reclaiming the connection between sexual expression, passion, love, and empowerment can be an act of creative resistance and resurrection. This reclamation helps deepen and illuminate the divine-human connection as one way to celebrate the Source of Life and God's intention for us, namely that of freedom, creativity, joy, and justice. This reclamation also embodies the prophetic biblical tradition that critiques those actions, institutions, and cultural arrangements that sexually distort or oppress.[13]

Furthermore, reclaiming the connection between sexual expression, passion, love, and empowerment as avenues for God's presence and joy in the world is deep within the Christian tradition, tracing back to Christianity's Jewish roots. Womanist theologian Kelly Brown Douglas argues that African religious heritage also views human sexuality as divine. She asserts that "those enslaved possessed a more accurate view of incarnation than their Western, free counterparts. . . . White culture's attacks on Black sexuality and its use of it as a tool of exploitation and oppression has effectively diminished Black valuation of sexuality."[14] This is one more piece of evidence of the ways in which colonization seeks to do violence. However, Douglas goes on to say, "the message of God's embodiment in Jesus is unambiguous: the human body is not a cauldron of evil but, rather an instrument for divine presence. It is the medium by which God is made 'real' to humanity through which God interacts in human history."[15]

---

13. James B. Nelson, *Body Theology* (Louisville: Westminster John Knox, 1992), 22.
14. Kelly Brown Douglas, *Sexuality and the Black Church: A Womanist Perspective* (Maryknoll, NY: Orbis Books, 1999), 113, quoted in *Shaping Sanctuary: Proclaiming God's Grace in an Inclusive Church*, ed. Kelly Turney (Chicago: Reconciling Congregation Program, 2000), viii–ix.
15. Douglas, *Sexuality and the Black Church*, 113.

Laughter, Song, Dance, and Worship as
Creative Acts of Resistance

One of my most important lessons about resistance and resurrection in the face of colonization came to me when I was eighteen. It was Christmas morning in 1987, and I was in the remote, mountainous Salvadoran village of Santa Marta as part of a small delegation of North American Christians and Jews representing the Accompaniment Movement.[16] We awakened, disoriented, to the ground shaking. Quickly, an older man who was a leader in the community explained that the Salvadoran government was dropping bombs nearby to scare and intimidate the residents of Santa Marta. The contrast between the ground-shaking bombs and the early Christmas morning was lost on no one. With such a backdrop, we heard more about the village's history, including the killing of this elder's daughter, who had been pregnant with her first child, and the murder of his childhood friend, who had been attempting to defend his own family. The elder described in detail the ways in which colonization targets real bodies with torture, pain, and death.

But the story made a sharp turn from the *Via Negativa* into the *Via Creativa* when, after describing the history, we sat in silence and prayed. Then he said, "Do you know how I can tell which North Americans are going to last here with us?" After a pause in which no one answered, he continued, "The way I know that anyone is going to last here is that they know how to laugh, to sing, to dance, to experience joy ... because the work we are doing is so difficult, we have to claim the promise of how the world is going to be, *now*. We have to live the promise. That's what our faith teaches us."[17]

This story foretells the importance of an inaugurated eschatology,

16. The residents of Santa Marta had, five years earlier, experienced a massacre—the Salvadoran National Guard had killed three thousand of the four thousand residents of the village. The remaining thousand people had fled to Honduras. Six weeks earlier, these survivors had walked home to the original site of their village, and our delegation had signed up to accompany them as a disincentive to the US-backed Salvadoran military to harm them. The disincentive came from the fact that in 1980, when four US churchwomen were killed, the US government had temporarily cut off aid to the Salvadoran government.
17. Salvadoran elder, interview by the author, Santa Marta, El Salvador, December 25, 1987.

which will be covered in much more detail in part 4. For now, it offers a glimpse of how laughter, song, and dance can be powerful tools of resistance and resurrection. Through them, those experiencing colonization can break the power-over dynamic by claiming their full humanity manifest in joy, now. Through laughter, they invert the bad to make it comical or playful. They can use the farcical for a dead-serious purpose, embodying the fact that colonization's defeat is already real because they are fully alive and free.

In her fictionalized account of the coup in Chile in the early 1970s, author Marjorie Agosín imagines the life of a teenage girl in search of her father, who has been "disappeared" by the military dictatorship. Her grandmother, her *abuela*, who is a survivor of Hitler's death camps, has urged her to have faith. So she strikes out with her friend after the dictator has died in search of her father.

> Am I crazy to try to find him? I look at Cristobal. "Were we crazy to come here?" I ask him. He tips his head back and laughs and laughs.
>
> "What? What? Cristobal!" I punch him on the arm. "Tell me!"
>
> "Ay, Céleste, of course you are crazy! Me, too. That is why we have always been friends. And that is why we will find your father. We are crazy enough to listen to silence, to see where there is nothing, and crazy enough, like your abuela always says, to have unshakable faith. Now let's walk."[18]

Cristobal and Céleste's ability to laugh is directly connected to their listening to silence, to their seeing what is not there, and to their unshakable faith. It is what propels them to live in hope and pursue justice. They, too, use their laughter as resistance and resurrection.

Within Christian communities, worship can be an important avenue of creative resistance and resurrection, especially when it employs these tools. In worship and ritual, we can create the time and space, if only momentarily, that approximate God's realm on earth. Worship, when done well, can help a community of people "to dream awake, to keep watch asleep, to live while dying, and to know ourselves already

18. Marjorie Agosín, *I Lived on Butterfly Hill*, trans. E. M. O'Connor (New York: Atheneum, 2014), 321.

resurrected!"[19] However, given the theological hegemonies that support colonization and populate much of the Christian tradition, such worship must be rooted in the kind of theological matrix this book suggests. It must consist of ritual, story, music, and sermons whose creativity, passion, and joy offer resistance to anything that seeks to colonize the body of Christ, the Earth-body, or our human bodies.

When worship and ritual are done in this manner, they become portals that carry us to places in which the real truth, about who we are and who God is, is experienced in palpable ways. They are dramas that help act out the dynamics of embodied justice and equity; they help us act out who we really are. Worship and ritual are forms of artistic creation, and when they are claimed as strategies for resistance and resurrection, they can transform not only individual and communal lives but also situations of colonizing violence.

Bernice Johnson Reagon tells the story of one such transformational moment:

The building was fairly remote—at least it is in my mind's eye. It sits on 106 acres of land in the mountains of Tennessee, set amidst trees. It was built in the 1930's. It was first home to classrooms for folks struggling to form a labor movement. But on this night in the 1950's, it housed a group of mostly African American and some other folks, learning the techniques of non-violent direct action in preparation for sit-ins across the Deep South. They were mostly young people sitting at desks and tables, studying and talking, making plans to help transform racist laws using their bodies and their lives.

As the sun went down on the Tennessee mountains, the smell of the settling dew came through the windows and the lights were turned on as the instruction continued. But at some point in the evening, another odor began to waft in. Something was burning. . . .

Before they knew it, the students of non-violence were surrounded by the epitome of violence. All around the building, members of the Klan stood, rifles and torches in their hands. As several burst through the door, they ordered the young people to the floor at gunpoint. Some in one room,

19. Esquivel, *Threatened with Resurrection*, 65. Permission obtained from Brethren Press editor, James Steetan, February 11, 2013, for use in this work.

others in another. And for what seemed like hours they lay there, hands over their heads, waiting for the shooting to begin.

But something happened that night. As the Klan stood with their guns trained on the young advocates of non-violence, someone began to sing "We Shall Overcome." And soon the song traveled to the other room until all were singing. As Bernice Johnson Reagon tells the story, the Klan didn't know quite what to do and time seemed to stand still as violence and non-violence met one another. As the verse ended, there was a pause until someone started a verse that had never been sung before. With the power of the Holy Spirit, a voice rang out "We are not afraid, we are not afraid, we are not afraid today. Oh, deep in my heart, I do believe that we shall overcome someday."

And then the sound of boots on the floor. And the sounds of doors closing. And the sounds of cars starting. And the Klan was gone.[20]

Toni Morrison offers another example of creating a moment in the realm of God through ritual, dance, song, and sermon. In her novel *Beloved*, she portrays a communal act of resistance to slavery and its accompanying theological racism. Baby Suggs, the spiritual leader of the community, gathers a group of former slaves whose bondage-into-freedom is an ongoing process. She has coaxed, prodded, and commanded them into a ritual of weeping, singing, and laughing in order to shed the hold of the colonizers. After they have ritually claimed their humanity, she begins to preach:

"Here," she said, "in this here place, we flesh; flesh that weeps, laughs; flesh that dances on bare feet in grass. Love it. Love it hard. Yonder they do not love your flesh. They despise it. . . . No more do they love the skin on your back. Yonder they flay it. And O my people they do not love your hands. Those they only use, tie, bind, chop off and leave empty. Love your hands! Love them! Raise them up and kiss them. Touch others with them, pat them together, stroke them on your face 'cause they don't love that either. You got to love it, you! And no, they ain't in love with your mouth. Yonder, out there, they will see it broken and break it again. What you say out of it they will not heed. . . . What you put into it to nourish your body they will snatch away and give leavins instead. No they don't love your mouth. You got to love it."

20. Bernice Johnson Reagon, "Convocation Address" (lecture, Earlham College, Richmond, IN, April 19, 1990), as told in Voelkel, "Highlander Singers."

"This is flesh I'm talking about here. Flesh that needs to be loved. Feet that need to rest and to dance; backs that need support; shoulders that need arms, strong arms I'm telling you. And oh my people, out yonder, hear me, they do not love your neck unnoosed and straight. So love your neck; put a hand on it, grace it, stroke it, and hold it up. And all your inside parts that they'd just as soon slop for hogs, you got to love them. The dark, dark liver—love it, love it, and the beat and beating heart, love that too. More than eyes or feet. . . . More than your life-holding womb and your live-giving private parts, hear me now, love your heart. For this is the prize."[21]

Through ritual and sermon such as the one Morrison describes, individuals and the community not only ground themselves in their liberated bodies, but they creatively dream and claim the reality of the *Via Positiva*. Thus, the *Via Creativa*, in solidarity with the *Via Positiva*, becomes an act of resistance against the *Via Negativa*. However, without the *Via Transformativa*, such resistance remains episodic and temporary. We need the *Via Transformativa* to help us point toward true and lasting liberation and life.

21. Toni Morrison, *Beloved* (New York: Penguin Group, 1987), 88–91.

PART IV

Via Transformativa—The Transformative Way

The *Via Transformativa* is the part of the matrix where the hope and promise of God's future break into our reality. It is rooted in and seeks to create a vision of what God's realm, on earth and in heaven, might look, feel, and taste like. It is an eschatological project because it professes that our dreaming about what liberated and decolonized bodies and sexuality might be (and our work to realize those dreams) is rooted in God's hope and promise. Such eschatological projects are always necessary, but they are particularly so when faced with the intransigence of colonization.

One moment in the Christian context in which the *Via Positiva*, the *Via Negativa*, the *Via Creativa*, and the *Via Transformativa* come together is that of communion. The congregation I served as pastor used these words as it practiced communion every week.

Words of Institution

We remember that on the night before Jesus was killed by those who feared him, he sat at table with his friends, women and men and children, sharing in the feast of the Passover, which is the celebration of the liberation of God's people. And remembering God's power, (take bread and break it while saying:) Jesus took bread, and after he had given thanks and blessed it, he broke it saying, "This is my work and my life, for you and with you. Take it all of you, and do this remembering me."

After dinner Jesus took the Elijah Cup, the cup that was traditionally reserved for the Holy One to come. (Raise the cup.) But instead of waiting, Jesus passed it to them as it is now being passed on to us, and he said, "This is the cup of the new covenant. It is the cup of justice and peace poured out for all. Drink of it, all of you, and do this remembering me."

Each time that we break bread together, we participate in the Body of the Risen Christ, for we are the Body of the Risen Christ. And each time we share this cup, we participate in the New Community for we are God's hope of the New Community. Let us consecrate these elements as we sing our table prayer together.[1]

Then, the congregation of mostly LGBTQ people, many of whom were dealing with addiction, were survivors of sexual violence, and/or were struggling with mental illness, came to the table and were served by clergy or lay people. After they were served, whoever had come together to the table would embrace and pray together, often through tears.

In it all is a clarity that God is about individual transformation but not only individual transformation. God is also about the liberation of communities and societies. The body of the risen Christ, having endured crucifixion, has been raised, and through communion, we are invited to participate together in this radical promise, realized in the present moment.

1. Spirit of the Lakes United Church of Christ, "A Service of Communion," in *A Place in God's Heart, A Place at Christ's Table: Worship Resources for the Welcoming Church Movement*, ed. David Lohman (Minneapolis: Institute for Welcoming Resources of the National Gay and Lesbian Task Force, 2007), 44–45.

7

The Already and Not Yet

Eschatology

Any constructive theological project that takes seriously women's and genderqueer people's bodies and sexualities is deeply eschatological. That is to say, the vision of how and what the world ought to be and how and what God's future holds forms the basis and inspiration for much of liberated, feminist, queered embodiment. Especially in a colonized context, an eschatological vision is necessary to discern what liberation, decolonization, and hope might look like.

Because in discussing the *Via Transformativa* I rely so heavily on eschatology, I want to be clear how my usage is similar or different from others. For theologians, eschatology is the systematic reflection on our Christian hope and what is at risk when we do not attain what our hope holds out to us. Eschatology has traditionally been focused on the "last things." But many Christians recognize that eschatology is more properly about the promised reign of God in all human experience and in all creation. It has powerful implications for both the individual and the community. Eschatology is not primarily concerned with what lies beyond death and outside of history. Eschatology is a practical and vital hope for the world as it is right now and in which we are all participating.[1]

This "here and now" eschatology fits well with a liberation, feminist, and queer understanding of eschatology. It roots our Christian hope in what God is doing to create a more just and liberated world. Nevertheless, precisely because justice is a major part of what we are hoping for, a sense of the timing and pacing of the eschaton is key.

Here, I am aligning myself with a tradition that celebrates an inaugurated eschatology as contrasted with a "realized" or "sapiential" eschatology on the one hand and "futuristic" or "apocalyptic" eschatology on the other. According to Jesus Seminar scholar John Dominic Crossan, both realized and future eschatology say "no" to the world as it is. In future eschatology, the world is negated and the stress is on imminent divine intervention: we wait for God to act. In realized eschatology, the world is also negated and the stress is on immediate divine imitation: God waits for us to act.[2]

By contrast, inaugurated eschatology says "yes" to the world but "no" to injustice. It recognizes both God's power and movement in human history and emphasizes our agency in response to that movement. Inaugurated eschatology lives in the tension and interplay of the already and the not yet.

Jesus's parables are full of pictures of what already-not-yet eschatology is like. They do not so much blueprint God's strategic plan as stir hope and sharpen wits to read the signs of kin-dom coming.[3] In the parables, we see Jesus telling stories that begin "the kingdom of heaven is like . . ." Taken together, Jesus's parables declare that God's kin-dom is surely coming because God cannot be defeated. They assure that appearances to the contrary deceive because kin-dom—like seeds and yeast—requires time to gestate and do its work in secret. Jesus's

1. Monika K. Hellwig, "Eschatology," in *Systematic Theology: Roman Catholic Perspectives*, ed. Francis Schüssler Fiorenza and John P. Galvin (Minneapolis: Fortress Press, 1991), 2:349.
2. John Dominic Crossan, *The Essential Jesus: Original Sayings and Earliest Images* (San Francisco: HarperSanFrancisco, 1998), 8.
3. I draw upon many of my pastors, including my mother, Rev. Marguerite Unwin Voelkel, who use the word "kin-dom" as a way to speak of the reality of God's presence fully realized without relying on the masculine king-dom.

parables exhort that we hope with boldness in spite of those things that look like setbacks (Mark 4:26–29; Matt 13:31–50; Luke 13:6–9; 13:18–30; 14:7–24). Jesus's preaching heralds the imminent arrival of the kin-dom. The kin-dom is not some far-off, unreachable time (Matt 4:17; 10:7; 12:28; Mark 11:10; Luke 10:9–11; 17:20–21). It is "in our midst," already really present in "the Jesus community," in the people of God gathered to read the scripture. The kin-dom is already "on offer" for anyone who is willing to accept it (Luke 19:11–27).[4]

Inaugurated eschatology calls on humanity to take an active part: to dream dreams of what is not yet but should be and, through the lens of these visions, to build up, recognize, and celebrate what is already really present among us. Inaugurated eschatology complicates our sense of time by forcing us to distinguish between what theologians call *chronos* and *kairos*. The Greek word *chronos* refers to chronological time, which orders events into a sequence: one thing after another. Chronological time orders the past before the present, which comes before the future. By contrast, *kairos* is God's time. *Kairos* does not order events in a sequence but interrupts chronological time with the inbreaking of God's presence, God's justice, and God's kin-dom. Inaugurated eschatology sees God's world in the tension and interplay between *chronos* and *kairos*. God is relentlessly acting in chronological time, behind the scenes in the hidden processes of history. Inaugurated eschatology sustains hope by recognizing *kairos* moments, when God's really present justice interrupts the sequence and breaks through in ways that wink (for those with eyes to see) or startle. This complex understanding of time helps us taste and feel and more fully understand the already-not-yet-ness of inaugurated eschatology. We, too, are called to do long-haul work, hidden and otherwise, to move along that arc of history that, we profess with confidence, bends toward justice. While it can be an excruciatingly slow process, the core of the gospel, the good news, is that God cheers us on with *kairos* moments of the kin-dom that assure us that the kin-dom of God is, indeed, in our midst.[5]

4. Hellwig, "Eschatology," 355.

Nothing brings out this *chronos/kairos* double-timing more than Luke's story of Jesus and the disciples on the Emmaus Road.

> Jesus himself came near and went with them, but their eyes were kept from recognizing him. And he said to them, "What are you discussing with each other while you walk along?" They stood still, looking sad. Then one of them, whose name was Cleopas, answered him, "Are you the only stranger in Jerusalem who does not know the things that have taken place there in these days?" He asked them, "What things?" They replied, "The things about Jesus of Nazareth, who was a prophet mighty in deed and word before God and all the people, and how our chief priests and leaders handed him over to be condemned to death and crucified him. But we had hoped that he was the one to redeem Israel." . . .
>
> . . . When he was at table with them, he took bread, blessed and broke it, and gave it to them. Then their eyes were opened, and they recognized him; and he vanished from their sight. They said to each other, "Were not our hearts burning within us while he was talking to us on the road, while he was opening the scriptures to us?" That same hour they got up and returned to Jerusalem.[6]

In this story, *kairos* interrupts *chronos* to move the disciples from the *Via Negativa* to the *Via Transformativa*. Christian communities reenact this episode at every communion service.

Several years ago, I preached a sermon on this text that highlights my understanding of God's *kairos* inbreaking:

> There are two things about our text that strike me. . . . The first is that the process of perceiving, of knowing, of seeing God's presence in human form took the disciples a minute. We don't know why, but they were kept from seeing Jesus for a while. Maybe because that's the way it often is for all of us. . . . They had to spend time together, Jesus had to draw out of them all the pain and trauma they had experienced, they had to journey a ways together in real relationship, they had to come out with their despair and longing and all they had hoped for. All of this had to happen before they could perceive him. And even more, they had to receive his teaching and entreat him to stay with them before their eyes were opened, in the midst of the simple, everyday, yet sacred act of breaking bread, and they recognized God incarnate, God enfleshed, God with them all along.

5. For a helpful exploration of *kairos* and *chronos*, see Ched Myers, *Binding the Strong Man: A Political Reading of Mark's Story of Jesus* (Maryknoll, NY: Orbis Books, 1994), 338–41.
6. Luke 24:15–33.

But that's not the only thing I read in this text. It's what happened next that also grabs my attention. And I need to thank the Rev. Felix Carrion for helping me see this through his sermon to the Minnesota Conference Annual Meeting. What happens after they perceive and recognize and grasp that Jesus has been with them all along is something miraculous.

Our text says, at THAT SAME HOUR, they got up and ministered. At that same hour, they were transformed by God's resurrection truth. Death had not won, God had. The torturers had not held sway, nor the Empire. The oppressors had not taken the day, God the liberator, God the maker of life out of death, God the deliverer had revealed the deepest truth. . . . Victory of life, joy of true transformation had won the day.

At that same hour, they got up in the recognition of resurrection power and they began their ministries. At that same hour, in the moment of recognition, they got up and returned to the place of their deepest despair to go into the streets of Jerusalem with a ministry of liberation.

My friends, we also live at that same hour. Because in God's time, the moment of recognition, of perceiving God's resurrection power, that moment delivers us from the oppressors' chains, from the Empire's plans, from the systems that would keep us in despair. At that same hour, those kindred in Christ who were training for non-violent direct action at the Highlander Center knew that violence can never rule the day and they sang out "We are not afraid." At that same hour, a small band of Congregational folks in New England had a vision that, because they were church people, they could not stand by as some human beings were enslaved in their own country, and the Amistad committee of the American Missionary Society, the precursor to one of the national ministries of the United Church of Christ, was born. At that same hour, someone here turned away from the demons of addiction and got in a car or on a bus or walked themselves into their first AA meeting in order to choose life and life abundant. At that same hour, some Farm Workers decided enough was enough and a young man named Cesar Chávez and a young woman named Dolores Huerta began to organize. At that same hour, over a lunch likely prepared by Mary, a motley crew of Activistas decided to join Centro de Trajabadores Unidos En Lucha and march against discriminatory proposed amendments on Minnesota's ballot. At that same hour, by the grace of God and through the power of this community, someone prayed and someone else sang and someone else's heart was broken open and began to heal.[7]

---

7. Rebecca Voelkel, "Timeless Time" (sermon, Lyndale United Church of Christ, Minneapolis, July 12, 2013).

These acts of glimpsing and grasping, and then claiming and creating God's eschatological promise of justice and liberation in the present time are a critical part of the *Via Transformativa*. Recognizing the inbreaks, claiming the promise of Divine justice, empowers us to embrace the *Via Positiva* and *Via Creativa* and encourages us to move forward toward that promised world that is the goal of the *Via Transformativa*. Recognition and action are both rooted in and producers of our Christian hope.

In 2011, nearly one thousand queer activists and religious leaders gathered to dream dreams and see visions. Their opening liturgy, at a conference called "Practice Spirit, Do Justice," captured the dynamics of eschatological vision and promise in a striking way:

> In the tradition of our elders, our forebears, some of whom we call saints, some of our best revolutionary thinkers, we want to hold and share with you the concept of a "third space," coming from black revolutionary activists in the south. If the first space is the conditions/the oppression we see and name, the second space is our reactions, our survival skills at their best, then the third space is where we dream. Practice Spirit, Do Justice, we hope, will be a third space.[8]

> Leader 1: We want to offer a third space, where we step back from the oppression and into the place where we allow ourselves to dream. . . . We have come to dream our collective liberation with you.

> Leaders 1, 2 and 3: We come together holding both the conditions of oppression and the possibilities for liberation.

> Leader 2: We come together because we believe that faith, spirit and building beloved community . . .

> Leader 1: will help us forge the trust we need to build bridges of solidarity.

> Leader 3: We come together because we dream of creating family and community rooted in individual and collective self-determination.

> Leaders 1, 2 and 3: We come to this third space holding the hope that we can do this work together with all of you.[9]

---

8. Sung Park, Lisa Weiner-Mahfuz, and Rebecca Voelkel, "Practice Spirit, Do Justice Opening Plenary" (lecture, "Practice Spirit, Do Justice: Creating Change Conference," Minneapolis, February 3, 2011).

The Gospels punctuate Jesus's ministry with "third space" episodes. One such third space comes in the story of Jesus's transfiguration. In the synoptic gospels, Jesus takes Peter, James, and John up on the mountain. Mark's gospel describes it as a "high mountain apart" (Mark 9:2b). In that space, which is geographically different (a mountain instead of a flat place) and spiritually different (they are apart from others and in prayer), Jesus is transfigured before the others and the barriers between time and space fall—Moses and Elijah appear and talk with Jesus. For a moment, Jesus, Peter, James, and John experience third space. In that space, God speaks, names Jesus "beloved," and commands the disciples to listen to Jesus. In that third space, the disciples receive both a glimpse of the future and instruction for how to live in the present.[10]

The *Via Transformativa* relies upon third spaces and moments in the realm of God where the eschatological promise is real, if only momentarily.[11] However, as the "Practice Spirit, Do Justice" liturgy above implicitly suggests, such eschatological visioning and creation of third space requires a high degree of intentionality. Dreaming and creating liberated and just spaces do not happen spontaneously. We are more likely to pay attention, and our dreams will be more apt to be justice dreams, if we are formed and prepared by one-day-after-another regular disciplines. The disciples had spent time with Jesus for a while before the inbreaking of the transfiguration and some more time before the interruptions of the crucifixion and resurrection. There was a context of preparation even though the interruptive inbreak took them far beyond what they might have thought they were preparing for.

The *Via Transformativa* requires of us similar preparation, so that we might more aptly pay attention, that we might more consistently dream justice dreams and not act out of false consciousness, that we might perceive the inbreak in our midst. Further, we must not act naïvely. We are indeed called to be lovers in the name of God but,

9. Ibid.
10. The story of Jesus's transfiguration is found in Matt 17:14–21, Mark 9:14–29, and Luke 9:37–43a.
11. Here I utilize "kin-dom of God" and "realm of God" interchangeably.

recognizing the power of the *Via Negativa*, things can go wrong. The *Via Transformativa* invites us to practice eschatological dreaming strategically and with care.

Embodied and Sexual Eschatology—Third-Space Rituals

Decolonized, liberated embodiment and sexuality require a high level of intentionality. Two examples illustrate both the importance of creating an embodied, sexual eschatology and the intentionality necessary to do so.

First: In order to engage in the practices of second and third space, more than one hundred First Nations women from all over the world were welcomed into a Maori cultural center in New Zealand in the late 1980s. They spent significant time naming and deconstructing the first space of their experience of colonization in each of their home settings.[12] They told stories and dreamed of what restoration of a life-giving third space might look like. Then, with great intentionality, they engaged in a ritual together.

After they had built significant trust, established protocols for the community that had gathered, and made themselves vulnerable to one another through stories and dreaming, they gathered in a ritual circle for a healing. One by one, as they were led, each woman disrobed and entered the center of the circle as the other women sang and danced. As she did so, others came and touched her body on all the parts that had been violated and abused. They touched her lips and her breasts, her vulva and her heart, her eyes and her feet. Anywhere there had been hurt, the collective body touched and brought healing. In the

---

12. Women of color experience significantly higher rates of sexual and physical violence. This is particularly true for First Nations women. Caught in the web of interlocking, colonizing realities of economic exploitation, sexual violence, racism, and Christian supremacy, many First Nations women hold in their bodies the scars of rape and abuse—both physical and spiritual. The figures from my research paint this painful reality. 77.3 percent of African American women and genderqueer persons who answered the survey reported being victims of sexual and/or physical violence; 66.7 percent of American Indian and Hispanic women and genderqueer persons reported the same data. For Asian American Pacific Islander women and genderqueer persons, the statistic was 57.9 percent. These figures compare with 46.3 percent of European American women and genderqueer persons reporting sexual and/or physical violence. All of this data comes from Voelkel, "Women, Our Bodies and Spirit."

language of the *Via Creativa*, it was not a pornographic circle but an erotic one. Its aim was not to bring arousal and climax but rather to banish the toxicity and pain of abuse and replace it with a sense of empowered embodiment and sexuality. Those present reported that, like the transfiguration, they glimpsed a future possibility and a vision of how to move in the world in the now.[13]

A second example of claiming an embodied, sexual eschatology comes from the Co-Madres in El Salvador. During the civil war in that country in the 1980s, thousands of women experienced the torture and death of their children. Some of them directly witnessed these atrocities. For most of them, the pain of violently losing a child whose life they had gestated was torturous. Initially, many of them reported being immobilized, but eventually, in an eschatological act of resistance and dreaming, they joined together to form a community.

One of the most important rituals these women reported was gathering together to weep over the loss of their children and spouses while they laid hands upon their own and one another's bodies. This ritual gathering was called a time of undrowning, and it marked a movement from pain and suffering into empowered solidarity.[14] After the women had undrowned themselves, they banded together in acts of protest or witness against the civil war. This experience illustrates what one gay African American theologian and activist says simply, "my people taught me that weeping can be the place where revolutions begin."[15]

Because decolonized, liberated embodiment and sexuality require a high level of intentionality, strategy, and care, it is important to emphasize these in the above examples. Each of the groups of women acted out of the deepest wisdom of their communities, paying close attention to the safety and vulnerability of each person. They understood that theirs were rituals of transformation, and so they took

13. Ku'umealoha Gomes, interview by author, Honolulu, June 17, 2000. Gomes is an indigenous Hawai'ian scholar.
14. They used the term *desahograr* (undrown) because by weeping they released the tears that were drowning them. Co-Madre of the Mothers of the Disappeared, interview by author, San Salvador, El Salvador, December 28, 1987.
15. Rodney McKenzie, March 20, 2015, Facebook post, http://tinyurl.com/jblfaye.

care not to reinscribe any experience of violation. Instead, permission and power was granted to each woman to decide to participate or not. It is also important to note that I do not share these stories here as a model of how others ought to act, rather as an example of culturally contextual and competent transformative practice.

Dreaming Dreams: Visioning in Practice of Sexual Eschatology

A third example of the importance of creating an embodied, sexual eschatology and the intentionality necessary to do so comes from my own organizing and pastoral experience. Over the years in "Sex and the Spirit" workshops, I have asked women and genderqueer people to craft their eschatological vision of sex, sexuality, and embodiment. Many begin with envisioning an end to colonization and ownership. For them, the end of ownership is both about property and about their bodies being owned by someone else. Dreaming beyond ownership allows them to grasp what empowerment, self-determination, and genuine negotiation might look like. Because ownership is so closely connected with jealousy (someone else is claiming that which is mine), moving beyond ownership then empowers some to envision a world without jealousy and power-over. This move often leads some women to envision polyamory, nonmonogamy, and a celebration of pleasure. For these women, ownership and monogamy are intertwined and decolonization, liberation, and hope are free of both.

For others, the safety of a monogamous relationship, which leads them to build a lifelong commitment, is the most decolonizing and liberative because the power dynamics and roles are stable and these allow for trust. Still others have noted that experimentation and play are important steps toward understanding their sexual eschatology.

The women and genderqueer people I surveyed made similar observations. Because I asked specifically about the respondent's genital sexual practice, the answers below offer a variety of explicit, direct answers. They are representative of the larger pool of over two hundred respondents. Some, epitomized by the following quote, needed to throw off what they experienced as colonizing ownership and practice promiscuity in the same way that I explored in the *Via Positiva* and *Via Creativa*.

> These days, parenting in a long-term relationship, we have lots of sex, I masturbate, we explore sex with other people, we want more than we have, I want more than I have, and I am ok.[16]

Others spoke of needing to stay open and see what kind of revelation came to them from their practice.

> Sex is the place where I get to play with instinct, with power and submission, with sensation and pleasure, with letting the ego sit to the side.[17]

For some, such as the transgender person whose response is included below, their sexual eschatology was more grounded in that particular part of their bodily identity.

> As a transgender woman, I find that my satisfaction in sexual activities comes from the effect I have on another person. I want to be the reason for another's orgasm: they find me attractive, they are aroused by me, and they climax because of me. That is my orgasm. I seldom have a physical orgasm—but I am emotionally and mentally fulfilled when my partner has a climax because of me. . . . There are times when I find myself extremely "turned on" by my feminine presence and can experience great fulfillment in having sex with myself. I have a friend who is bisexual and was attracted to me as something between man and woman. He is married and his wife is approving of his having affairs outside of their relationship as long as there is no threat to her—he can't have a relationship with another woman. After some time together sexually, he had to stop the relationship because he no longer could see me as anything other than a woman—and a woman with whom he had great, erotic, satisfying sex. And as such a woman, I was a threat to his marriage. He thought I would be devastated but I was thrilled that I had reached that epitome of feminine attractiveness—I had an orgasm.[18]

For many, the vision of a transformed world begins with individual transformation and moves to loving and claiming the gift of body in all

---

16. Voelkel, "Women, Our Bodies and Spirit."
17. Ibid.
18. Ibid.

its particularity and context. This includes monogamous genital sexual practice as well as other forms of embodied intimacy. Three survey respondents offer the following, which add to the stories above:

[As an African American] I enjoy/love being a woman, love monogamy, love [having] sex with a person I am in love with. I enjoy intimacy.[19]

[I'm a] heterosexual, monogamous (married) [woman], and [have] a predictable sex life—that is what feels safe for me. My husband is 10 yrs older and does use Cialis, but even so, I like to know a day ahead of time that sex is coming so that mentally I can prepare. There is no spontaneity, but it is a satisfying intimate relationship. I just have to be really intentional about letting go and enjoying sex.[20]

I have sex with one partner, my only partner. We have been together for 26 years. Sex is still good after all these years. I can't imagine being this intimate with anyone else.[21]

The measure of liberation in sexual eschatology is found in self-determination, explicit and honest negotiation about power, articulated and mutually agreed-upon boundaries, and ongoing dialogue. In the face of what the *Via Negativa* shows us of the creation of soul-crushing, exploitive, power-over colonization, these practices—which emphasize the personhood, subjectivity, and sacredness of each person and are rooted in the *Via Positiva* and *Via Creativa*—are the markers of liberation in a sexual eschatology. Additionally, because the powers that the *Via Negativa* requires us to confront seek to destroy connection, empathy, and shared carnal knowledge with God and one another, a liberated sexual eschatology emphasizes the corporate, connected body whose longing and desire is to be in just community with one another. It is because of this context that negotiation, which requires support and feedback between partners, is critical. Such negotiation and shared discernment claim the reality that in a relationship, there are the individual bodies of each partner, which are incarnational, and there is the "body" that

19. Ibid.
20. Ibid.
21. Ibid.

is the relationship itself. The communal body that is created because of the sexual/love relationship is incarnational in similar ways to the communal body of a group of people gathered for worship. It, too, points us to God's presence and God's carnal knowledge of humanity, and it must be honored as such. The responses presented above illustrate that women's and genderqueer people's dreams and hopes may vary widely while still holding up the goals and ideals of liberative eschatology.

Many lesbian feminist scholars nuance an even more a communal understanding of the *Via Transformativa*'s eschatological vision of sexuality and embodiment. They affirm the reality of more than genital expression. For many of these scholars, an embodied and sexual eschatological vision requires a theology of friendship that expands the definition of sexuality and embodiment. These theologians take the above-articulated experiences and expand upon them. For Mary Hunt, one of the most important markers of women's sexuality is that it is defined by mutuality, community, honesty about sexuality, nonexclusivity, flexibility, and other-directed-ness.[22] For Audre Lorde, the eschatological vision is similar: empowerment, creativity, liberation, and community are as important as genital communion.[23] For both Lorde and Hunt, it is not enough simply to dream as individuals; rather, the project of a sexual and embodied eschatology must be done in community, where it is open to the critique and dialogue of others. Such communal dialogue promotes a clarity of vision for the individual's eschatological dreaming; it also allows for the reality of the shared and communal body's sexual and embodied eschatology. It helps in the present moment because it helps each person be creative and not crazy as s/he lives against the grain of colonization.

Further, this points toward the *Via Positiva*'s affirmation that the

---

22. Mary E. Hunt, "Lovingly Lesbian: Toward a Feminist Theology of Friendship," in *Sexuality and the Sacred: Sources for Theological Reflection*, ed. Marvin M. Ellison and Kelly Brown Douglas, 2nd ed. (Louisville: Westminster John Knox, 2010), 169–82.
23. Audre Lorde, "Uses of the Erotic: The Erotic as Power," in Ellison and Douglas, *Sexuality and the Sacred*, 75–79.

incarnation is not only present through the life and ministry of Jesus, nor only in the individual bodies of people. Instead, the incarnation is also present in the honest, faithful efforts at just and loving relationships that friends, families, communities, and societies make. These communal bodies are vital parts of the body of Christ. As the next chapter suggests, such communal bodies, dreaming together on an ongoing basis, are critical if we are to move from individual dreams to building a movement for a transformed world.

Power and Eschatological Visioning

The tension, however, remains for many between the *Via Negativa* and the *Via Transformativa*. Many survey respondents and people in the "Sex and the Spirit" workshops speak of the difficulty to dream. One such respondent stated it this way:

> My relationship with sexuality would be easier if I were a cisgendered man. I am very aware of the condemnation of queer people both in the faith community of my birth and by my current denomination. I think my generation is more ready to see a positive relationship between sexuality and spirituality than past generations, but we're not there yet and it's hard to stay in relationship with older members of my faith community and ethnic group while holding such a position. While I hunger for an embodied spirituality, I find myself conflicted. I reject gender essentialism that does not seem to fit with my identity nor life experience. I am not fully at home with my body and how others perceive it so this does not fit with a sort of mind-body oneness that I might otherwise embrace. I find Galatians 3:28 to be the most important verse in the Bible to me.[24]

This illustrates the importance of the practice of dreaming, of the need for communal support and the degree of intentionality necessary to foster such a practice. Unfortunately, many people struggle with this exercise precisely because of their theological upbringing within a colonizing and hegemonic tradition. Consequently, it becomes crucial that such work be done in a theological context that both seeks

---

24. Gal 3:28 reads: "There is no longer Jew or Greek, there is no longer slave or free, there is no longer male and female; for all of you are one in Christ Jesus." The rest of this quote comes from Voelkel, "Women, Our Bodies and Spirit."

liberation and decolonization *and* is communal and creates accountability. This is necessary because the destructive forces of the *Via Negativa* that require our awareness are real. And even as we are seeking the *Via Transformativa*, we can have bad dreams, perverse dreams, abusive dreams, colonized dreams. To claim the *Via Transformativa*, we need to develop the safeguards and disciplines that prepare people to be dreamers of transformational dreams. And, when we take wrong turns, places and spaces that allow us—as individuals, communities, and movements—to repent, make turns, and return to the center of things.

In order to create such safeguards and disciplines, we must return to an analysis of power and how power operates to oppress and liberate. Table 2 (below) illustrates both the colonized reality that grants power to some individuals and communities and creates vulnerability in others. Table 2 also illustrates that the *Via Negativa* and its colonization are not the whole of the story. Eschatological visioning—for individuals and in community—empowers resistance and resilience, creates accountability and checks and balances to bad dreams, and creates third space.

	Sources of Power[25]	Sources of Vulnerability	Sources of Resistance/Resilience/Accountability
Age	Adult	Child, teenager, or elderly	Gray Panthers, Griot Circle, other empowered elders in community[26]
Race	White	Person of Color	Community of empowerment as a person of color
Sex	Male	Female/Intersex	Feminist/womanist work
Economic Class	Wealthy	Poor	Queers for Economic Justice[27]
Education	Holding a degree	Holding no degree	Lifelong learners
Ability	Physically and mentally able-bodied	Having a mental or physical disability	Accessible-to-All Movement, Sins Invalid[28]
Sexual Orientation	Heterosexual	Gay, lesbian, or bisexual	Welcoming Religious Movement[29]
Gender Identity	Cisgender[30]	Transgender or genderqueer	TransSaints, TransTorah[31]

The power of these communal bodies, of these communities of resistance, accountability, and resilience, is evidenced throughout this work. The First Nations women who formed the healing circle and

25. This grid is adapted from Voelkel-Haugen and Fortune, *Sexual Abuse Prevention*, 6. I have added "Sources of Resilience/Resistance" at the urging of many of my colleagues.
26. The Gray Panthers and the Griot Circle are both organizations devoted to the activism and community by, for, and about elders and older people. http://www.graypantherstwincities.org/ and http://www.griotcircle.org/.
27. Queers for Economic Justice is an organization working to support the lives of queer people who are working class, poor, or economically oppressed. http://www.queersforeconomicjustice.org/.
28. The Accessible to All Movement in the United Church of Christ is a movement of disability justice activists working with and within churches and communities to amplify the gifts of people living with disabilities. http://tinyurl.com/zb54d35. Sins Invalid is a performance project that incubates and celebrates artists with disabilities, centralizing artists of color and queer and gender-variant artists as communities who have been historically marginalized. http://www.sinsinvalid.org/.
29. For a clearinghouse for information about Welcoming Church Programs, visit http://www.welcomingresources.org/.
30. Cisgender is a term to describe those persons whose gender identity aligns in the way society proscribes to their biological sex. For example, those who identify as men born with a biological sex of male.
31. TransSaints invites trans people of faith to become involved in leadership and advocacy training that is focused on the unique perspectives of the African American trans community. http://www.transsaints.org/. TransTorah helps people of all genders to access fully and transform Jewish tradition, and helps Jewish communities to be welcoming sanctuaries for people of all genders. http://www.transtorah.org/.

reclaimed their individual and communal body is a community of resistance, accountability, and resilience. The Co-Madres who undrown themselves is another. The Act-Up artists whose ethical spectacle claimed their own humanity and the humanity of those living and dying with AIDS is yet another. In each of these, it is a gathering of those whose individual identity is composed mostly of sources of vulnerability. But when these individual bodies allow themselves to gather in the spirit and power of resistance and resurrection, they become a communal body that empowers, inspires, and claims the already nature of the eschatological promise.

The story with which this chapter began illustrates that Christian worship, when done with intentionality, can be such a community of resistance, accountability, and resilience. Communion, when practiced as a rite of liberative eschatology, can be the sustenance of such communal bodies. Preaching, singing, and praying can be the dreaming that allows us to build third space, to experience collective moments in the realm of God, and to more closely incarnate the body of the risen Christ.

8

Eschatological Strategies: "Movement-Building" Wisdom as a Test Case

Where eschatological projects are concerned, it is important that those who dream dreams and see visions are realistically rooted in an analysis of power and strategic action. Happily, movement-building theory can offer us a framework that will enable us to be self-conscious and intentional about how power works so that we can partner with God to transform the world in more savvy and wise ways. As such, I believe that movement building is the evangelism to which the church is called.[1] In other words, the good news that Christians are called

---

1. There is a whole realm of academic study devoted to the construction, success, and failure of social movements. In my role as the Faith Work Director for the National Gay and Lesbian Task Force, my colleagues and I employed different portions of social movement scholarship in order to help us work more faithfully and effectively. In particular, I would point to Lisa Weiner-Mahfuz, a former racial justice staff colleague at the National Gay and Lesbian Task Force, who has helped me understand the ways in which intersectional justice, movement building, and spiritual and religious communities are deeply intertwined. Her thinking and blogging around intersectionality and other movement-building topics can be found at: http://intersectionsconsulting.wordpress.com/.

to proclaim needs to be embodied as eschatological action for social transformation.[2] One of the primary reasons I utilize movement-building wisdom is that I believe progressive Christianity is a movement and that it will both grow and be much more authentic and powerful if it understands itself as such.

Movement-building theory has many different facets. Three of them are important for our purposes: the Grassroots Policy Project's analysis of the "Three Faces of Power," the relational quality of movement building, and the long-term nature of the work.

Three Faces of Power

According to the Grassroots Policy Project's model, for a social movement to grow and successfully transform society, it must recognize and utilize power in three different yet interrelated ways.[3] They name these "Create and Disseminate a Worldview," "Build an Infrastructure," and "Wage Campaigns / Mass Mobilization." Their interplay can be visualized in this way:

2. Although I am applying movement-building wisdom to religious work, there is nothing about it that is inherently religious. However, as I hope will be clear in this chapter, movement-building wisdom has much to offer our religious movements for justice.

3. Grassroots Policy Project, *The 3 Faces of Power*, February 2007, PDF, http://tinyurl.com/hh5dma7.

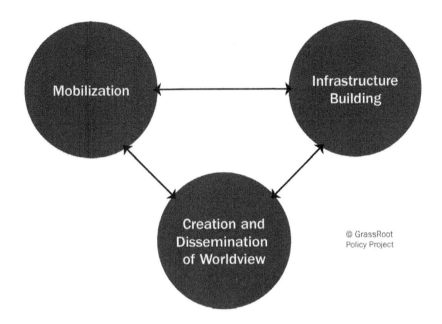

Figure 2

The Faces of Power and the Welcoming Religious Movement

It will be easier to understand these ideas if we work with concrete examples. Mine come from the movement with which I am most familiar, the Welcoming Religious Movement. From 2005 until 2013, I served as the faith work director for the National Gay and Lesbian Task Force.[4] In that role, I worked closely with hundreds of pro-LGBTQ religious colleagues.[5] Together we put this theory into practice

---

4. The National Gay and Lesbian Task Force renamed itself the National LGBTQ Task Force in 2014.
5. While any list I would write would be incomplete, it is important to name some names here, because any movement owes its lifeblood to the real, genuine, and sacred relationships between people and communities. I was called to this role by the Welcoming Church Program Leaders, which included Emily Eastwood, Tim Feiertag, Rev. Carol Wise, Rev. Troy Plummer, Rachel Harvey, Dr. Michael Adee, Dr. Patrick Evans, Rev. Alex McNeill, Rev. Ann B. Day, Donna Enberg, Rev. Malcolm Himschoot, Rev. Ruth Garwood, Gwen Thomas, Andy Lang, Rev. Ken Sehested, Rev. Ken Pennings, Rev. Robin Lunn, Kerry Armstrong, Dr. Mark Johnson, Rev. Rob Williams, Rev. Shari Brink, Marilyn Paarlberg, Rev. Dr. Sally Harris, Meredith Bischoff, Sharon Troyer, Renee Waun, Justin Lee, Max Niedzwiecki, and David Cupps. I soon had the honor of facilitating the National Religious Leadership Roundtable and co-facilitating the Bishops and Elders Council, whose combined membership included nearly one hundred pro-LGBTQ religious organizations and later, those who facilitated the "Practice Spirit, Do Justice" conference. Among my most important colleagues and teachers were Bishop Yvette Flunder, Rev. Elder Nancy Wilson, Rev. Mike Schuenemeyer, Dr. Joel Kushner, Rev. Debra Haffner, Chris Paige, Rev. Dámaris Ortega,

strategically in order to grow the movement for inclusion and justice for LGBTQ people within their own religious traditions and the larger society.

The historical beginnings of the Welcoming Religious Movement are many. One root is found in the collaboration between LGBTQ people who are affiliated with LGBTQ organizations and straight-identifying religious clergy working to bring about change in societal laws. The first such example of this is the Council on Religion and the Homosexual (CRH). CRH was a collaboration between progressive Christian clergy and leaders of "homophile" organizations in San Francisco. In a historic first, the Glide Urban Center of Glide Memorial Methodist Church convened a retreat in 1964 of fourteen representatives of the Daughters of Bilitis, the Mattachine Society, the Tavern Guild, and the League for Civil Education, and sixteen progressive Christian clergy leaders from Methodist, Quaker, Episcopal, Lutheran, and United Church of Christ denominations. This led to the formation of the Council on Religion and the Homosexual (CRH). A police raid on a CRH-sponsored dance at California Hall on January 1, 1965, thrust CRH into the public spotlight. In the immediate years following, CRH was at the forefront of educating religious groups and leaders about homosexuality and generating religious support for legal and social reforms for homosexual people.[6]

Another root of the Welcoming Religious Movement is the formation of predominantly LGBTQ denominations and congregations. In 1968, the Reverend Troy Perry founded the Universal Fellowship of Metropolitan Community Churches (MCC) as a predominantly LGBTQ denomination. Other predominantly LGBTQ / same-gender loving denominations within Christianity have been founded since then,

Lisbeth Melendez-Rivera, Rabbi Joshua Lesser, Idit Klein, Faisal Alam, Urooj Arshad, Imam Daayiee Abdullah, Rev. Jakob Hero, Carol Lautier, Rev. Dr. Jonipher Kwong, Lisa Weiner-Mahfuz, Sung Park, Bishop Tonyia Rawls, Lisa Anderson, Dr. Bernie Schlager, Rev. Dr. Jay Johnson, Rev. Dr. Roland Stringfellow, Bishop Joseph Tolton, Louis Mitchell, and Beth Zemsky. In particular, Rev. Harry Knox, Dr. Sharon Groves, Macky Alston, Ann Craig, Ross Murray, and Dr. Sylvia Rhue took time every month to be both a community of support and accountability.

6. LGBT Religious Archives Network and GLBT Historical Society, "Clergy and Homosexual Persons Converge in San Francisco: Dialogue," The Council on Religion and the Homosexual exhibit, LGBT Religious Archives Network, accessed May 19, 2015, http://tinyurl.com/z27gzp5.

including Unity Fellowship Church Movement (a predominantly African American denomination founded in 1982 in response to the AIDS epidemic) and the Fellowship of Affirming Ministries (a predominantly African American Pentecostal ministry founded in 1999).

Examples of predominantly LGBTQ congregations include BCC (Beth Chayim Chadashim), founded in 1972. It was so named to show respect for MCC, from which the founders, a group of Jewish people who were attending MCC, came. Since that time, a wide variety of predominantly LGBTQ congregations have grown within different religious traditions. In addition to Beth Chayim Chadashim, there are several predominantly LGBTQ synagogues that are affiliated with either the Reform, Reconstructionist, or Renewal movements (Congregation Beit Simchat Torah in New York, Congregation Sha'ar Zahav in San Francisco, Congregation Kol Ami in Los Angeles, Congregation Or Chadash in Chicago, and others). There also now exist LGBTQ dharma meditation circles (like Queer Dharma) and Muslim retreats and prayer circles (through the work of such organizations as Muslims for Progressive Values and the Muslim Alliance for Sexual and Gender Diversity).

A third root of the Welcoming Religious Movement is that of "welcoming congregations" within larger denominations. Within Judaism, there is both a formal Welcoming Synagogue project as well as less coordinated efforts to help individual congregations welcome LGBTQ people within Conservative, Reform, Reconstructionist, and Renewal movements. (One interesting reality for work within Jewish communities emerged from a large survey of Jewish congregations from the five major movements. It found that only 10 percent of LGBTQ Jews are partnered to other Jews, and many of those families have children of color. Therefore, for work around LGBTQ welcoming, advocates have had to also support congregations in creating a policy of welcome for interfaith relationships and justice for Jews of color.)[7]

---

7. Steven M. Cohen, Caryn Aviv, and Ari Y. Kelman, "Gay, Jewish, or Both? Sexual Orientation and Jewish Involvement," *Journal of Jewish Communal Service* 84, no. 1/2 (Winter/Spring 2009): 160.

Within Christianity, there has been a movement to create welcoming congregations since the early 1980s. Found in many denominations and fostered through ecumenical collaboration, the Welcoming Church Movement is a vibrant subset of the Welcoming Religious Movement. Starting in the early 1980s, Welcoming Church Programs have grown the number of welcoming churches from none to nearly 5,500. Within Hinduism, there are several examples of welcoming communities. Kashi Ashram in Florida is a prominent one.

A fourth root of the Welcoming Religious Movement is the work done to change policy and culture within denominations. There exist nearly one hundred pro-LGBTQ religious organizations, whose foci often include increasing the numbers of welcoming congregations and communities and changing the policy and/or culture of their larger denominations/religious communities. Examples include More Light Presbyterians, the Brethren Mennonite Council for LGBT Interests, the Muslim Alliance for Sexual and Gender Diversity, Keshet, and the Pagan Alliance.

Face of Power: Creation and Dissemination of a World View

The first "Face of Power" to be discussed here recognizes and utilizes cultural beliefs, norms, traditions, histories, and practices to shape meaning. What this means for the liberation movements I have been exploring is this: our eschatological vision needs to be expressed in a way that connects it to the larger context of world view. World view includes the ways in which people understand the world around them, their roles in that world, and what they see as possible. The dominant and hegemonic world view in early twenty-first-century US culture reinforces a kind of rugged individualism—a go-it-alone, bootstraps approach—that discourages involvement in collective action. The inaugurated eschatology about which I dream and for which I believe we must act is not just about individual transformation, or even community transformation. Rather, it demands of us nothing less than harkening to the realm of God. In order to engage this bodacious, outrageous task, we must be inspired by the vision of an interrelating

Via Positiva, Via Creativa, and *Via Transformativa* as they give us the fortitude and wisdom to withstand and resist the forces we encounter through *Via Negativa.*

Because any social movement is a competition for meaning, the struggle between the dominant, hegemonic world view and the eschatological vision/world view described in this work is very important. It is of central importance. The dominant, hegemonic world view is encountered, identified, and resisted in the *Via Negativa.* This world view draws upon colonizing binaries and seeks to uphold the dominant/submissive system, which violently extracts from many to enrich the few. The vision articulated here, that we are called to be lovers in the name of God, is one in which power and resources are shared, multiplicity is honored, and God's carnal knowledge of our individual and communal bodies is celebrated. While other faces of power are vital, the making of meaning and shaping of world view is of paramount importance in building a movement that genuinely transforms systems and cultures.

Some successful ways of creating and disseminating such an eschatological vision include: shaping ideas and the way people make sense of what they see and hear; linking work in the shorter term to a broader vision and long-term goals; challenging the current dominant, hegemonic world view's emphasis on rugged individualism, competition, and the limited role of government; and framing issues with common eschatological themes so they are integrated together and reflect an alternative vision.[8]

Religious traditions intuitively do work in this Face of Power. As I illustrated in part 3 on the *Via Creativa,* good worship is an opportunity both to set the vision of how the world ought to be and to inspire the collective body to dream and act toward that reality. The Welcoming Religious Movement has considered work within this Face of Power to be vital. While I served with the United Church of Christ Coalition for LGBT Concerns, we began to speak and write about "God's Extravagant Welcome" as our world view.[9] It both captured our vision around

8. Grassroots Policy Project, *3 Faces of Power.*

LGBTQ justice and spoke to the core values of the United Church of Christ. Coming out of the AIDS epidemic and the rejection many African American LGBTQ people experienced both from white LGBTQ people and African American church leaders, Unity Fellowship Church Movement chose as their guiding vision, "God is Love and Love is for Everyone." For many Jews who do pro-LGBTQ justice work, the language they use is "Tikkun Olam." Tikkun Olam means "Repair of the World" and suggests that humanity has the responsibility to heal, repair, and transform the world. Like the deeply culturally competent world views of the United Church of Christ and Unity Fellowship Church Movement, Tikkun Olam articulates core values and communicates the vision of how the world ought to be in ways that are Jewish and honoring of LGBTQ people.

There are many, many other examples of the ways in which world-view Face of Power work has been done brilliantly in other movements. One current example of this is the Black Lives Matter movement. Faced with hegemonic, colonizing dehumanization that treats black and brown bodies as disposable, the vision that "black lives matter" is both a vision of how the world ought to be and a strategy for present work. Created by queer black women who sought to respond to the murder of Trayvon Martin, it is both a vision of justice and a claiming of the present sacredness of black and brown bodies and lives.

Another Face of Power: Building an Infrastructure

The next Face of Power to occupy us emphasizes building deeper infrastructure within organizations, congregations, judicatories, committees, denominations, and their grassroots members, and creating ties with other kinds of organizations, such as think tanks, multifaith gatherings, councils of churches, and advocacy groups. Here are some examples of building and using the second Face of Power:

• building sustained membership involvement in congregations,

---

9. The United Church of Christ Coalition for LGBT Concerns is now the Open and Affirming Coalition of the United Church of Christ.

communities, and denominations, and organizing people for collective action

- developing leaders who can guide our congregations, communities, organizations, and coalitions

- building and maintaining coalitions, councils of churches, multifaith organizations, alliances, and other forms of collaboration

- seeking to expand the agenda by bringing in new communities and constituencies to help develop and support a bold, new progressive Christian and multifaith agenda that unites different issues[10]

In the context of this work, the second Face of Power might be seen as nurturing the bones, muscle, and connective tissue of the communal/ movement body. This Face of Power is one manifestation of the reality that God has carnal knowledge not only of individual bodies but of humanity's collective relationships and gatherings.

From the beginning, the Welcoming Religious Movement has put considerable effort into work in this Face of Power. The harvest has been plentiful. There are now nearly 100 pro-LGBTQ religious organizations, 5,500 welcoming congregations within Christianity, hundreds of welcoming synagogues within Judaism, nearly forty welcoming prayer circles within Islam, countless welcoming pagan and Wiccan circles, many welcoming dharma circles and *sanghas*, and many other multifaith welcoming spaces. These are a testament to the Welcoming Religious Movement's work in this Face of Power: building infrastructure. In addition to these "bones and skeletal systems," a movement also needs coalitions and "connective tissue" to make it viable. Some of the most interesting and exciting work done within the Welcoming Religious Movement has happened in those connective, coalitional spaces. These include:

- The National Religious Leadership Roundtable (NRLR), started by Urvashi Vaid of the National Gay and Lesbian Task Force in 1998. It

10. Grassroots Policy Project, *3 Faces of Power*.

is composed of nearly 100 multifaith pro-LGBTQ organizations and religious leaders. Over the years, the NRLR has met for strategizing, made numerous public statements on political and religious issues, and organized members for action around ballot initiatives (such as a 2007 campaign in favor of a transgender-inclusive anti-discrimination measure in Connecticut, a 2008 campaign against California's Proposition 8, and a 2010 campaign in Puerto Rico to gather religious support for LGBTQ equality and justice).

• The Bishops and Elders Council consists of nearly thirty pro-LGBTQ Christian organizations, intentionally gathered to focus on the intersections of Catholic, Protestant, Pentecostal, and Evangelical, and the ways in which LGBTQ, racial, and economic justice interweave. Co-founded by the National Gay and Lesbian Task Force, DignityUSA, the Universal Fellowship of Metropolitan Community Churches, and the Fellowship of Affirming Ministries, this coalition has been meeting since 2006.

• The Welcoming Church Program Leaders have been meeting since 1991. Representing thirteen Welcoming Church Programs within Protestant contexts, this coalition shares a relational-organizing training program called "Building an Inclusive Church," which equips leaders to direct their local congregation through a welcoming process. Their primary goal as an organization is to increase the numbers of welcoming congregations within the denominations in which they work.

• The Religion Council has been convened by the Human Rights Campaign and consists of multifaith religious leaders who engage in public theology or leadership. They strategize and advise the Human Rights Campaign's Religion and Faith Program as well as participate in different campaign actions.

• Additionally, there are multiple one-time convenings of pro-LGBTQ religious leaders and campaigns for which multifaith or ecumenical partnerships are created—on the local, regional, or national levels. Examples include the Faith Organizing Roundtable, a multifaith gathering of representatives from twenty-five different traditions that planned and executed work within each tradition and in multifaith partnership in order to first defeat an anti-marriage-equality amendment in Minnesota and then successfully advocate for marriage equality in the Minnesota legislature from 2011 to 2013.

Face of Power: Mass Mobilization / Campaign

Social movements typically focus much of their energies on another Face of Power: organizing through mass mobilization to change laws and policies, to impact elections, and to affect political and economic decisions. Social movements often measure success by how well they impact elections and how well they influence decision-makers in legislatures, courts, General Synods, General Conventions, General Conferences, Vatican Councils, Annual Meetings, and corporate boardrooms. Activities used to exercise this Face of Power include:

- trying to win issue campaigns—including passage of support for LGBTQ people, opposition to the death penalty, support for women's ordination, and many other examples

- helping candidates (such as legislators, congressional leaders, presidents of denominations, presiding bishops, head rabbis, bishops, and presbyters) get elected to office

- taking legal action—engaging in direct action: strikes, petitions, and accountability sessions, including within our denominational and religious traditions

Work in this Face of Power—mass mobilization—has been evident within the Welcoming Religious Movement since its inception. As the example of the Council on Religion and the Homosexual suggests, pro-LGBTQ religious people have been organizing for just laws in a myriad of settings. However, in the context of a dominant hegemony that purveys homophobia, biphobia, transphobia, and heterosexist religion, coalitions between pro-LGBTQ religious organizations and "secular" pro-LGBTQ campaigns have been complicated. The cultural and political success from the religious right (who are primary proponents of the dominant hegemony) combined with the many pro-LGBTQ secular activists whose personal narratives involve throwing off repressive religious traditions resulted in deep suspicion of pro-LGBTQ religious activism. Particularly in the late 1990s and for much of the 2000s, many campaigns that involved LGBTQ issues, such as nondiscrimination or marriage equality, intentionally shied away from religious coalition building or messaging.

I ran into this dynamic myself when I was working on the "No on Prop 8" campaign in California in 2008. I was convening the National Religious Leadership Roundtable (mentioned above) at the time and we chose to meet in San Francisco. As part of our meeting, we held a press conference to which we invited over 100 multifaith clergy, including the head pulpit rabbi in San Francisco from the Reform tradition, the ELCA bishop, the UCC conference minister, the Episcopal bishop, and a leading Wiccan priestess. No fewer than four different No on Prop 8 organizers called me to try to deter us from holding the press conference because polling had shown that "moveable middle" voters "didn't want to see 'religion' fighting." The No on Prop 8 campaign had interpreted this data to mean that pro-LGBTQ religious people needed to keep quiet because the Yes on Prop 8 campaign had rooted all of their work in religious language and communities.

My experience highlights not only the difficulty in doing pro-LGBTQ campaign work from a religious context. It also brings into clearer focus the importance of doing work in all three Faces of Power and what happens when work in all three Faces of Power has not happened. Because there had not been enough, or effective enough, work in infrastructure building—forming secular/religious coalitions prior to the Proposition 8 campaign—the relationships and trust were not present during the mass mobilization work on the No on Prop 8 campaign.[11]

11. To the credit of both the pro-LGBTQ religious and secular organizers, much reflection, debrief, and analysis went into the failures of the No on Prop 8 campaign. I wrote one such analysis following a two-day debrief between secular and religious leaders. See Rebecca Voelkel, *A Time*

However, there have been significant shifts in the pro-LGBTQ campaign landscape in the last decade. This is due to many factors. Among them is the success of the Welcoming Religious Movement's movement-building work. In the world view creation and dissemination Face of Power, the Welcoming Religious Movement has been increasingly successful in disseminating the kind of liberating world view articulated in this book, which has begun to disrupt the hegemonic and deeply oppressive world view that the religious right has been disseminating for decades. Other factors include deep and good work in the other Faces of Power within and amongst different religious traditions, work that has been going on for years but is reaching critical "tipping points." In work on the infrastructure-building Face of Power, the forty-plus years of pro-LGBTQ religious organization building, thirty-plus years of organizing welcoming congregations and communities, and twenty-five years of working in ecumenical and multifaith coalitions are blossoming into concrete shifts and gains. Additionally, work on the mass-mobilization Face of Power done within religious traditions includes countless campaigns to change religious denominational policy, thousands of ethical spectacles (such as forming "choral gauntlets" through which voting delegates have to walk), and ecumenical and multifaith delegations sent to the World Council of Churches and the Parliament of World Religions. All of these have built the intrareligious pro-LGBTQ movement and significantly transformed the religious landscape. They have also laid important groundwork for a new collaborative spirit between secular pro-LGBTQ campaigns and pro-LGBTQ religious people.

However, as evidenced in the Religious Freedom Restoration Acts, which sought to justify and baptize discrimination as religious (read: Christian) freedom, passed in various states in the past few years and seen in the 2016 election cycle, the power of colonization to reassert

---

to Build Up: Analysis of the No on Proposition 8 Campaign and Its Implications for Future Pro-LGBTQQIA Religious Organizing (Minneapolis: National Gay and Lesbian Task Force, 2009). The successes of 2012 and beyond owe much to the time spent learning from the mistakes of 2008.

itself must never be underestimated. Eschatological movement building must always be vigilant and persistent.

A Fourth Face of Power: Personal Transformation / Healing Justice

The Grassroots Policy Project's Three Faces of Power model gives us an important start. But the conditions of marginalization that cry out for justice movements to transform them reveal a significant missing piece. Marginalized individuals and communities lack access to systemic resources. They are the targets of fear and hatred, degradation and belittlement. Marginalized individuals and communities experience high rates of violence and trauma, such as sexual abuse, beatings, intimidation, killing of peers or family, or the threat of these. Constant rejection by those in authority because of their marginalized status is another marker of the conditions of marginalization.

Two concurrent issues spring from these conditions of marginalization:

- Those in marginalized communities can perpetrate horizontal violence and oppression. That is to say, they can hurt one another rather than work against the systems of oppression that cause the conditions of marginalization. They can harm their leaders, peers, colleagues, and other members of marginalized groups (either their own or those similarly situated).

- People in marginalized communities can also injure themselves. They can hurt themselves by driving or pushing themselves and those around them in inhumane ways. This can take the form of unrealistic work schedules and hours, never taking Sabbath time or rest, and clinging desperately to success at all costs.

In the face of such realities, activists and theologians have begun to talk about the need in social justice movements for a fourth Face of Power, that of "personal transformation or healing justice."[12] This fourth Face of Power correctly realizes that for any movement to be successful over the long haul, in order to genuinely move out of oppression into liberation, it must support spiritual and emotional health and healing—for individuals and by creating a culture of healing, spiritual maturity, and communal, embodied justice. The *Via Creativa* already sensitizes us to this wisdom. Just as the Salvadoran elder predicted the success of North Americans in his midst by their ability to dance, sing, and laugh, so the fourth Face of Power recognizes that healthy movements need to be able to claim third space. They need to be able to nurture communities of resistance and resilience in which individual and communal empowerment, healing, and joy are felt and experienced.

Figure 3 illustrates the four Faces of Power:[13]

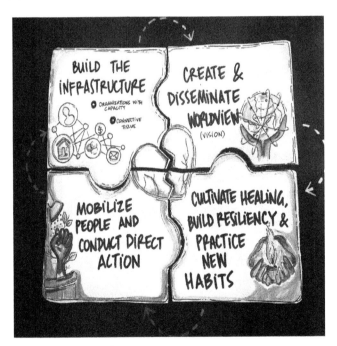

Figure 3

12. Ashley Harness, "Spiritual Care for Justice and Wholeness: A Case Study for LGBTQ Movement Building" (master's thesis, Union Theological Seminary, 2012), 10. I also want to highlight the work of Lisa Anderson and the Sojourner Truth Leadership Circles. She has articulated very well the importance of Healing Justice.

13. I created this graphic to illustrate the integration of the Grassroots Policy Project's Three Faces of Power with the fourth Face of Power.

In part 2, on the *Via Negativa*, I explored colonization and its validating theological hegemonies and the conditions of marginalization and oppression expressed in horizontal violence and self-injury. One of the ways in which the *Via Transformativa* is realized is through an individual's and/or community's reclamation of the *Via Positiva* and *Via Creativa* through the transformation of the fourth Face of Power. Additionally, twin dangers confront social movements that ignore the fourth Face of Power. The first threatens from within in the form of internal power struggles, both organizational and among individuals. Its characteristic symptoms include illness, depression, exhaustion, and burnout. The second danger comes from without as opponents seek to exploit the vulnerabilities within the movement.[14] For example, dominant theological hegemonies often seek to create a good/bad binary within oppressed groups. Those who are "good" follow the mores, behaviors, and theologies of the dominant culture and are called a "credit to their [race/gender/sexual orientation/gender identity]." They are contrasted with the "bad" of the oppressed group, who resist, rebel, or embody a different theology, protocol, or culture than that of the dominant hegemony. If a social movement is comprised of members who have not engaged in personal transformation or done work around their own embodied or sexual eschatology, they can become victim to the dominant hegemony's divide-and-conquer, good/bad binary strategies. However, if the fourth Face of Power is included in movement building, great fecundity and possibility emerge with a comprehensive picture of individual, communal, and systemic work.

Within the Welcoming Religious Movement, there are a myriad of examples of fourth Face of Power work. It could be argued that many of the Welcoming Religious organizations to which I refer began as spaces for healing and personal transformation. Many of the early gatherings

14. An example of this is the news that the National Organization for Marriage used a strategy to draw a wedge between Latinx and African American communities and the LGBTQI community. However, if work can be done around the fourth Face of Power, such attempts would backfire because the presence and power of Latinx LGBTQI people and African American LGBTQI people would help prevent this. See Michelle Goldberg, "National Organization for Marriage Memos Reveal Racial Wedge Strategy," *The Daily Beast*, March 27, 2012, http://tinyurl.com/jjk8nnb.

of LGBTQ and same-gender loving people were for retreat and safe space in which to undrown and heal. And today, as new organizations start their work, they often do so in the context of healing retreats. For instance, one of the most important parts of the work of the Muslim Alliance for Sexual and Gender Diversity is their "Retreat for LGBTQ Muslims and Their Partners." Another important part of this work of personal transformation and healing justice involves the need to engage and heal the trauma and grief, sometimes so deep as to be cellular, that LGBTQ people and communities have endured.

Just as the convening of First Nations women, mentioned in the previous chapter, involved a sacred ritual of touch in order to recognize, grieve, and heal the epidemic of sexual violence indigenous women experience, so there exists such a need within LGBTQ communities. Particularly for transgender people, in particular transgender women of color, the rates of violence, including murder, are overwhelmingly high. Every year on November 20, nearly two hundred cities around the world mark Transgender Day of Remembrance; the names of those transgender and gender non-conforming people who have been murdered are read, candles are lit, and then stories of pain, survival, and healing are told and borne witness to. In recent years, many cities have added to their Transgender Day of Remembrance rituals, which have pointed toward and claimed healing as a necessary and important part of remembering those who have been killed.

Deepening Our Understanding of Faces of Power Work

As I have noted above, each of the Faces of Power is critically important, but if taken in isolation from one another, they fail to effectively build a movement. It is the interplay, interrelating, and simultaneity of the work in all Faces of Power that is critical. Whether engaging in the healing Face of Power or the mobilization Face of Power, the world-view Face of Power—ability to articulate what we work toward and fight for—is a key part of any social movement. But if we are only dreaming and preaching about an embodied and sexual

113

eschatological vision, without any ability to manifest action, we are not engaging in movement building. If all we do is engage the second Face of Power (infrastructure building) by garnering members for our organization for the sake of numbers and budgets but do not inspire them to transformational healing and action, we are mired in the dominant hegemony not eschatological evangelism.

Instead, when a campaign is underway, it ought to be intentionally disseminating a particular world view or narrative (not just talking points) and it ought to be intentionally helping to build and strengthen relationships between organizations and people for the longer term. As healing retreats happen, their organizers ought to be thinking about the systemic changes needed to transform the lives of those whose healing they desire. As coalitions gather, they ought to be creating their shared visions, the protocols of how they will work together in humane and transformational ways, and what actions or ethical spectacles they can engage in that will further their work in the other Faces of Power.

The success of the Welcoming Religious Movement is one testament to this simultaneous, interrelated Faces of Power work. They have taken the infrastructure-building Face of Power seriously by engaging in significant leadership development and training—such as the Building an Inclusive Church program, which teaches relational organizing and movement-building skills. In turn, these individual leaders are a community together and have been activated to lead their own congregations through a welcoming process. Once their own congregations have made the journey, trained people mentor and support other congregations in the welcoming process. Such a process is a campaign (the mass-mobilization Face of Power), but the Building an Inclusive Church program makes it clear that the Face of Power that is vision and world-view dissemination, deeply rooted in the particular culture of the congregation, is critical for any welcoming process. Amidst a welcoming process, retreats, healing services, and rituals are often utilized. Thus, all four Faces of Power are present when a welcoming process is done well. As mentioned above, since the early

1980s, nearly 5,500 congregations have made this "welcoming" journey.

Building this network of welcoming congregations has had a deep impact on secular contexts as well. In the example of the Faith Organizing Roundtable in Minnesota, it was to the nearly 150 welcoming congregations within Minnesota that the secular campaign turned, and these congregations served as one pillar of their religious efforts. And it was to the nearly three hundred pro-LGBTQ religious leaders that the Minnesota campaign also turned for world-view dissemination. These welcoming communities and clergy were in online videos, music videos, and print advertisements making the case for the legality of love.[15] World-view Face of Power work was happening amidst mobilization Face of Power work. Those congregations and clergy who were identified for their interest and participation in the campaign but were not officially rostered as welcoming by their denominations were contacted and led through the rostering processes. Thus, infrastructure-building Face of Power work happened amidst mobilization Face of Power work.

Implicit in the above examples is that the "power" of which Faces of Power speaks is both political (in that it relates to our secular political system) and cultural (in that it relates to the mores, languages, styles, and ways of being that exist in relationship to the political system but are much larger than the political system). For those of us in religious communities, we recognize that we operate in relationship to both the political and cultural understandings of power because religion significantly impacts both. Furthermore, when pro-LGBTQ religious leaders use this information, we also note that our religious communities are very political systems. Hence, in the examples above we see that the wisdom of the Faces of Power model also applies to building movements within our religious, political systems.

15. One particularly moving example of this was the work of Catholics for Marriage Equality who used a song written by David Lohman for the Welcoming Church Movement called *For All the Children* and made it into a music video: Catholics 4 Marriage Equality, "For All the Children . . . Vote 'No' in November in Minnesota," YouTube video, 6:25, posted August 16, 2012, http://tinyurl.com/gqxqwe9.

Relationship as Central to Movement Building

Central to all of the above is a commitment to the sacred within each person. This commitment serves as a measure of effective movement building. Within the Welcoming Church Movement, which is a subset of the Welcoming Religious Movement, this commitment is called "graceful engagement." In Building an Inclusive Church training, participants are taught that relationship building is at the center of the movement for inclusion and justice for LGBTQ people, and the relationships that are built are founded on the practice of engaging each person in a community as if they are a beloved child of God. One profound example comes from a Lutheran church in Columbus, Ohio.

> The Church Council was debating whether or not to begin a welcoming process. For three consecutive months at the Council meeting, the motion was tabled as an older mother of a gay son and a young father with young kids argued endlessly. At the end of the third Council meeting, the older mother invited the young father to meet the following Sunday after worship in the narthex. She invited him to bring a picture of his family. At the time of their appointment, she arrived with a single picture of her family, he with a grocery bag full of pictures of his.
>
> For fifty-five minutes, he shared picture after picture of his family and told stories. She listened and asked questions. With five minutes left of their time together, she shared her picture and pointed out her son and his partner.
>
> What emerged from their meeting was that the young father was overwhelmed with his responsibilities as a dad. He had no family near-by and relied heavily on his church family for support. He was fearful a welcoming process would take away what he considered to be desperately-needed support from his family. The older mother asked if she might serve as a grandmother to his kids and he gratefully accepted. When the next Council meeting came around, he had not transformed to being a flag-waving pro-LGBTQ person, but he was able to stand-aside and let the process begin.[16]

This story is often told as a profound example of the importance of

---

16. Rebecca Voelkel, Vicki Wunsch, David Lohman, and Tim Feiertag, *Building an Inclusive Church: A Welcoming Toolkit* (Minneapolis: National Gay and Lesbian Task Force, 2013), 3.

graceful engagement and the transformative role that listening as a means to building relationships can play. Central to the story is the older mother's realization that debating and argumentation were not transforming anyone, nor getting her closer to her desire to engage her church in a welcoming process. She also understood that coming to know her "opponent" had the potential to transform both of their lives. And she knew that offering the gift of listening was an important first step to building a relationship. This wisdom—moving away from debate toward listening and relationship building—is key to building a movement of lovers in the name of God.

Long-Term Nature of Movement Building

Another key element of movement building is the reality that this work takes time. While I was critical of the No on Prop 8 campaign for the lack of competency with religious communities, it is also true that infrastructure-building Face of Power work—building relationships of trust that are rooted in genuine knowledge of one another—does not happen overnight. The fact that strong secular/religious partnerships did not exist during that campaign was, in some part, due to the fact that genuine relationship had not been formed. In order to form real relationship, as opposed to transactional ones, time needs to be spent, experiences shared, and commitments witnessed.

This long-term nature of movement building is one of the hardest pieces to reconcile for activists, funders, and community members alike—especially those of us who live amidst the capitalism of the United States. This dominant economic culture demands instant results, proof of short-term success, and evidence of immediate effectiveness, all of which make long-term work appear untenable. But the desire for immediate change also springs from those who work toward economic, political, and social transformation. People are suffering now: colonization is destroying lives in every moment that passes. This sense of urgency in transformative practice can fuel action. But effective movement building requires revolutionary patience and eschatological hope, too. Without them, liberation efforts are doomed to failure. With them, we have hope of real change. Two examples help illustrate this:

• The Abolitionist movement had many roots, but by the time of the American Revolution, efforts were afoot in many of the colonies/states to stop the importation of new slaves and abolish slavery altogether. Nevertheless, countless hours of organizing were spent by millions of people and hundreds of thousands of lives were lost before the end of the Civil War and the passage of the Thirteenth Amendment to the Constitution in 1865 brought the legal end of slavery. As is evidenced above, this legal end to slavery has not ended racism in this country. Generations, including our own, have had to continue the work to engage and transform what has been called one of America's original sins.

• The Seneca Falls Convention to discuss the social, civil, and religious condition and rights of women was organized in 1848. Thousands of gatherings, tens of thousands of dollars, and millions of conversations later, Women's Suffrage passed in 1920. The success of this campaign does not indicate the success of the movement. Much work remains to be done. (The election cycle of 2016 and the resurgence of white nationalism show the deeply intractable qualities of racism and sexism, and many other interlocking, colonizing forces. They are a powerful example of the enduring quality of the *Via Negativa* and the need for strategic, long-term movement building.)

As we explore the long-term nature of movement building, one more piece of nuancing is necessary. It is important to recognize the complexity of time to which I pointed earlier in part 4 on the *Via Transformativa*. The long-haul nature of movement building is largely a function of *chronos*. But amidst this patient, carefully relational work, *kairos* can break in. When this happens, movement builders refer to "catalyzing events." As I have been writing this book, one such "catalyzing event" has happened in the movement for racial justice. The Associated Press describes it this way:

> The Confederate flag was lowered from the grounds of the South Carolina Statehouse on Friday, ending its 54-year presence there and marking a stunning political reversal in a state where many thought the rebel banner would fly indefinitely.
>
> The turnabout seemed unthinkable before the June 17 massacre of nine black parishioners—including a state senator—at a Charleston church during a Bible study. Dylann Roof, a white man who was photographed with the Confederate flag, is charged in the shooting deaths, and authorities have called the killings a hate crime.[17]

For effective movement building to happen, diligent, relational, strategic efforts must happen within chronological time. Then, when *kairos* breaks in, movement builders must recognize this inbreak and respond. In many ways, the work within *chronos* can be seen as preparation for the *kairos* moments that we know will come.[18]

But there is one more layer of movement-building wisdom that informs our eschatological project and helps nuance our understanding of time and timing.

---

17. Jeffrey Collins and Meg Kinnard, "After 54 Years, Confederate Flag Removed from Statehouse," Associated Press, July 10, 2015 10:31 a.m.
18. When Rev. Dr. Jann Cather Weaver preached at my installation as pastor at Spirit of the Lakes United Church of Christ on November 16, 1997, she suggested that the Micah 6:8 text that reads "Do justice, love kindness and walk humbly with your God" might be better translated, "Do justice, love kindness, walk prepared with your God."

9

This Historical Moment—Recognizing the
Signs of the Times

Movement-building wisdom urges us to work in all four Faces of Power, to do so in deeply relational ways, and to recognize that time and timing are critically important to the success of the work. In order to ensure that we work as strategically as possible as lovers in the name of God, we need to take chapter 8's information and deepen our understanding of the role of the world-view Face of Power.[1]

This Face of Power is all about our dreams for the world as it ought to be. But our world view does not only offer us a vision of the future, it gives us a lens through which we also view the present and interpret the past. One of the world views from the previous chapter can help illustrate the power and importance of world view. If we understand the dream to be "Tikkun Olam/Repair of the World," then we likely value what heals and transforms in the present. We likely judge those things that wound or break people and relationships as wrong. In many

---

1. Much of the thinking I present in this chapter owes its genesis to my friendship and collegiality with Beth Zemsky. She has been my mentor, teacher, and conversation partner as I have sought to apply the thinking shared in this chapter.

ways, our world view becomes the lens through which we view and understand the world.

When assessing the strength or effectiveness of any movement, it is possible to measure how much the world view of a given movement is resonating with people in society. Do people use the language of the world view or assume its vision as they speak? What percentage of society uses the movement's language? How often does the language or its assumptions appear in print, social media, worship, art? These all help to determine the resonance of a particular world view.

The resonance of a particular world view with a society's population can be visually represented by "waves," akin to either sound waves or waves in the ocean. How much a world view resonates builds over time, hits an apex, and then decreases into a nadir. The distance between one valley or nadir and another represents the life cycle of the resonance of a particular world view. The valley is the beginning of a world view's resonance, when it begins to "bubble up" and people in a variety of places start to coalesce around and utilize the language. As more and more people start to assume the world view and refer to it, organize their work around it, and share the dream, the resonance wave line rises until it reaches its apex. At that point, a majority in the culture are utilizing the language of the world view, even if they disagree with it.

An example is useful to illustrate the point.

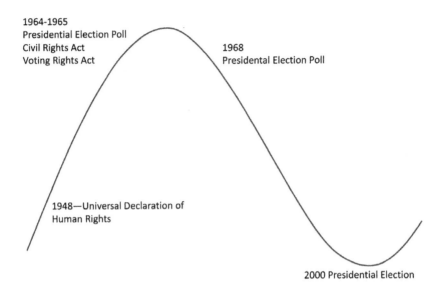

1964-1965
Presidential Election Poll
Civil Rights Act
Voting Rights Act

1968
Presidental Election Poll

1948—Universal Declaration of
Human Rights

2000 Presidential Election

Figure 4

The world view of the last progressive-movement wave was that of "rights." Born out of many of the struggles of the 1920s, the idea that every human being deserved a certain set of rights that allowed for a decent life and brought dignity and respect began to emerge as a shared dream and vision around which people were beginning to coalesce and congregate. By 1948, we saw the Universal Declaration of Human Rights and much of the postwar rebuilding of Europe under the Marshall Plan was framed in this language. In the United States, we experienced the growth of the Civil Rights movement, with its vision utilizing "rights" language and imagery. By 1964–68, the apex of the resonance of the rights vision, presidential exit polling found that the American electorate understood "rights" as the number one issue facing the country. By 1972, "rights" as an issue or vision was number eight in presidential exit polling. By 1976, it was sixteenth, and then it disappeared as the primary vision in the electorate's mind.

This does not mean that the issues for which people were working no longer included the understanding of the dignity and worth of individual people. It does mean that work in the world-view Face of

Power—sharing the vision of a world in which everyone enjoyed certain rights—was no longer the most meaningful way to describe it. It also means that, as the world view or vision of rights stopped resonating, it was harder to do work in the other Faces of Power. In other words, as the resonance of the world view rose and reached its apex, more people were involved in organizations and coalitions that dreamed the dream of rights, more people were able to be mobilized for action, and more aspirational policy goals could be achieved. For example, 1964–68 marked the apex of the resonance of the vision of rights because the Civil Rights Act of 1964 and the Voting Rights Act of 1965 were passed during these years. Additionally, as the rights vision was rising and at its apex, other movements adopted its vision, such as the women's rights movement, the gay rights movement, and the environmental rights movement. But then, as the resonance of the world view waned, membership in organizations declined, it was harder to mobilize people, and aspirational policy goals diminished or disappeared.

The waning of the resonance of the progressive-rights world view coincided with the rise of the conservative movement and the resonance of its world view. Such is the inverse relationship between the waves of world-view resonance. As the progressive-rights world view experienced the apex of its resonance from 1964 to 1968, Barry Goldwater suffered a huge loss in the 1964 presidential election. In response, a group of leading Republican leaders, strategists, and operatives began meeting to regroup and strategize. What emerged was a movement-building plan whose brilliance and success is a beauty to behold—something I must admit even as I vehemently oppose the results. Over the course of the next forty years, their plan unfolded in near pitch-perfect fashion. It can be loosely traced this way:

- 1965–75: formation and work of think tanks on the world-view Face of Power: discerning, testing, creating, and beginning to disseminate a world view of individualism, security, and values

- 1970s: infrastructure Face of Power work through the formation of organizations such as the Christian Coalition, the Institute for Religion and Democracy, and the Moral Majority

- 1980s: mobilization Face of Power work through local school board elections, whose real purpose was to disseminate and hone world view and build the lists of organizations. Additionally, with Ronald Reagan in the White House, the conservative world view also gained a powerful voice, as did initiatives such as fighting communism and fighting a "war on drugs," which laid the groundwork for imprisoning people of color at astronomical rates and, eventually, for gutting many of the Civil Rights movement's gains.

- 1990s: the beginning of the rise in the resonance of the conservative world view and the 1994 "Republican revolution" with Newt Gingrich in leadership. Even though Clinton, in the White House, was a Democrat, he was compelled to operate within the growing world view of the Right, including welfare reform and the Defense of Marriage Act (which both highlights the need for security against the "threat" of same-sex marriage and a particular set of "values").

- 2000s: the election of George W. Bush represents the apex of the resonance of the world view of the Right—security, individualism, and values. With the 9/11 attacks as a catalyzing event, it was possible to implement aspirational policy goals such as the Department of Homeland Security, whose mission is "to secure the nation from the many threats we face"; the Patriot Act of 2001 (subsequently renewed); and the Intelligence Reform and Terrorism Prevention Act of 2004.

- 2016 election cycle and the election of Donald Trump also traces its success to the successful movement-building on the Right. Even as the worldview is past its apex, the infrastructure of talk-radio, cable television, and the so-called "alt-right" was key to the mobilization efforts that resulted in Trump's election.

While these are very broad brushstokes, they illustrate how the rise of the resonance of the Right's world view corresponds with the growth and effectiveness of the conservative movement. The visual representation of this growth and the inverse relationship between the resonance of the progressive world view of rights and the conservative world view of individualism, security, and values is represented below.[2]

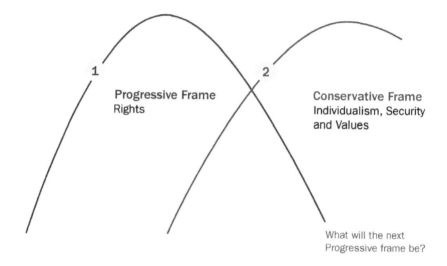

Progressive Frame
Rights

Conservative Frame
Individualism, Security
and Values

What will the next
Progressive frame be?

Figure 5

Framing

On a community level, it is important to connect the larger world view of a movement and the values and mores of the group of people with whom you work. This connection is accomplished through a "frame." For example, in the Welcoming Church Movement the tenor, spirit, and feel of a welcoming process are key. Utilizing the relational approach of graceful engagement, the goal is to present a welcoming process in a way that resonates with a congregation's core values and faith, using language and images that call on the best in the church's life. This approach "frames" the process.

A frame can be thought of like a picture frame. Just as a picture frame can either bring the beauty of a piece of art into clearer focus

2. Beth Zemsky and David Mann, "Building Organizations in a Movement Moment," *Social Policy* 38, no. 3 (Spring/Summer 2008): 14.

or distract so much as to interfere with its beauty, so the frame any community chooses to do its justice work can either facilitate or disrupt the work. An example from the Welcoming Church Movement helps illustrate the importance of framing.

A Simple Cup of Coffee[3]

A Lutheran church in the Midwest was not an official Welcoming Congregation, but they were very clear that they highly valued hospitality. They wanted a concrete way to demonstrate that hospitality, something that went beyond just words, a handshake, and "here's a bulletin." So they set up a barista stand in the narthex. The first thing you encountered as you walked into their building was a friendly face offering to make you a free cup of whatever you'd like.

The congregation was playing host to a fundraising concert, and among the performers was the local Gay Men's Chorus. One Chorus member was a man who had been deeply traumatized from his time in the church; an experience all-too common within the LGBT community. After taking the courageous step to leave the church years before, he vowed, in an act of self-protection, that he would never set foot in a church again.

However, because of this upcoming concert, he was now being placed in an impossible bind, torn between that vow he'd made years earlier and his commitments as a member of the Chorus. But somehow, he found the courage to show up at the church for rehearsal. But think about the emotional state that he must have been in—the mix of fear and courage, defensiveness and vulnerability—as he walked up those stairs, approached the door, and paused for a moment before finally pushing the door open and walking inside.

The first thing he encountered was that friendly face behind the counter saying, "Welcome. Can I make you a latte?" That simple act of hospitality reached through that painful jumble of emotions and so deeply touched his heart that he started to cry. The person behind the counter, a bit puzzled by these tears, had no idea about the emotional journey that man was on, nor the healing power of that simple offer of coffee.

When the congregation later learned of this story, they quickly decided to embark upon a Welcoming Process. And it was abundantly clear that "hospitality" would be their frame. This was such a successful frame for

---

3. Voelkel et al., *Building an Inclusive Church*, 34.

them because—*in a single word*—it succinctly summed up their most deeply held values and who they saw themselves to be.

World View Resonance, Framing, and This Historical Moment

As I explore the relationship between articulating an eschatological vision of liberated and decolonized embodiment and sexuality, the wisdom of social movement theory, and the task of building the world envisioned in this work, it is important to note that many movement-theory leaders believe we are just at the beginning of the next progressive "wave."[4] If that perception is accurate, and I believe it is, a new world view or frame is about to emerge. But since there exists an inverse relationship between conservative and progressive waves, there is much work to be done if we are to build and organize the kind of movement I have described: one grounded in an eschatological vision of liberated and decolonized embodiment and sexuality for individual bodies, for the communal body, and for the global body.

Resonance of World View and Specific Movement-Building Tasks

One of the most practical and helpful parts of the movement-wave theory is that as the resonance of the world view grows or wanes, there are particular tasks for movement builders to complete and particular emphasis to be placed upon the work for one or more of the Faces of Power. When the world view is just emerging and the resonance is low, movement builders need to spend most of their energy on activities related to the world-view Face of Power—listening to what is emerging from a variety of decentralized places, talking with those whose values and dreams are shared, and experimenting with what is "sticking" with folks—and on activities around the infrastructure-building Face of Power, such as determining which individuals share the analysis and passion to serve as core members of the movement. Additionally,

---

4. January 23–27, 2013, saw more than three thousand progressive activists gathered for the "National Conference on LGBT Equality: Creating Change." In numerous workshops, plenary sessions, and private conversations, there was agreement with Zemsky and Mann's conclusion that we are in a "movement moment," one in which the next progressive wave is beginning.

the beginning of the resonance wave calls upon movement builders to help with collective identity development within the movement. For instance, in the LGBTQ movement, collective identity was the result of a move away from behavior—men having sex with men, women having sex with women, or language about being "homosexual"—toward a cultural identity of being "homophile," "gay," "lesbian," or "queer." This is the process by which individuals begin to understand their identities as empowered and tied to a particular movement.

As a world view is gaining resonance, activities accelerate around the infrastructure-building Face of Power, even as dissemination of the world view continues to be key. These are times for deep work in coalition, building the membership and capacity of organizations, convenings, and so forth. Mass-mobilization Face of Power activities are important as the resonance of the world view is growing (as the growth of the conservative movement shared above illustrates) but not necessarily in order to win. Instead, these campaigns have as their goal sharing the world view and building the network and relationships within the movement. It is when the resonance of the world view reaches its apex that aspirational policy goals are much more likely to be achieved and campaigns won. There are also specific actions to be taken as the resonance of the world view wanes. These are all illustrated below:[5]

5. Beth Zemsky, "Netroots Pre-Conference Intersectional Meeting of Multifaith Leaders" (presentation, Netroots Conference, Providence, RI, June 6, 2012).

1 Framing, Base-building
   Collective Identity

2 Developing Infrastructure

3 Mass Mobilization
   Aspirational Policy Goals

4 Professionalization and Interest Groups

5 Reactive Organizing

6 Movement Maintenance

Figure 6

Implications for the Project of Embodied, Eschatological Hope

As I have dreamed a world where all are lovers in the name of God, movement-building wisdom has been a critical tool in the practice of the *Via Transformativa*. It has been the place to which our ancestors turned to help them build the Abolitionist movement and the Women's Suffrage movement. It has been the place to which the leaders of the Civil Rights movement returned again and again as they sought discernment of their next step. And as I have worked with colleagues in the LGBTQ religious movement, movement-building wisdom has been the primary tool of evangelism as we have sought to proclaim the good news of an embodied, eschatological hope.

Given the movement-wave theory presented in this chapter, we know we are at the beginning of the next progressive wave. This moment in the development of world-view resonance calls on us to do work on discernment and the creation of a new world view and on gathering together the core of the new movement. These "signs of the times" are one reason I have such excitement about all that I have shared here.

This project is an attempt at good theologizing. Good theologizing is always important. But good theologizing is also good work in the world-view Face of Power. And good theologizing that is also world-view Face of Power work, done in close partnership with movement builders and rooted in a church that cares about transforming systems of colonization and injustice, is desperately needed in this moment.

I am excited about what I have shared in this book because of what seems to be emerging as the next world view. In multiple meetings, conversations, religious and secular conferences, and strategizing sessions, the emerging progressive world view seems to be about interconnectedness, interdependence, and common good—those things that emphasize human dignity and collective connection.[6] This attempt at good theologizing has tried to take seriously the intersections, the connective tissue, the interdependence, the collective body. As such, I am hopeful it can be a resource in this movement moment.

Summary of Movement-Building Wisdom

The movement-building wisdom articulated in this and the previous chapter is an extraordinary tool for a concrete, embodied eschatological project like this one. Deeply aware and responsive to this historical moment and drawing on the relational, long-haul four Faces of Power knowledge explored above, we can create a movement of lovers in the name of God that is

- guided by an embodied and sexual eschatological vision of liberation and decolonization;

- manifest in congregations, communities, denominations, and

6. I want to be clear that this is ever evolving and not yet determined, however much work is being done to listen and experiment and reflect back on what the emerging frame might be. This is of particular relevance to religious communities, given the critical role that spiritual and religious people and communities play in creating and disseminating a vision, inspiration, and world view.

organizations that are practicing deep connection to one another through both support and accountability, and are populated by personally transformed and transforming individuals;

- acting collectively in creative, courageous, resurrection-claiming, promiscuously incarnational ways;

- rooted in genuine relationships that harken to that of God in all people; and

- practicing revolutionary patience even as they are prepared for and awaiting the inbreaking of the kin-dom.

Such a movement makes me joyful! And it strikes me as a worthy goal for those of us who claim to be heirs of the prophets who call us "to do justice, to love kindness, and to walk humbly with your God" (Micah 6:8). We heirs of the prophets remind one another that, in Carter Heyward's eloquent words,

> To love you is to make love to you, and with you, whether in an exchange of glances heavy with existence, in the passing of the peace we mean, in our common work or play, in our struggle for social justice, or in the ecstasy and tenderness of intimate embrace that we believe is just and right for us—and for others in the world. To love you is to be pushed by the power/God both terrifying and comforting, to touch and be touched by you. To love you is to sing with you, cry with you, pray with you, and act with you to re-create the world.[7]

This understanding of the *Via Transformativa*—dreaming an embodied and sexual eschatology and building a movement that is both rooted in those dreams and responsive to the moment in which we live—is one articulation of how we both carry the legacy we have been granted and pass to the next generation a legacy of great value.

---

7. Heyward, "Sexuality, Love and Justice," 301.

Conclusion

In 2012, my family and I spent a lot of time working against a ballot initiative in our home state, Minnesota, that would have amended the state constitution to define marriage as being only between one man and one woman. Our daughter, who was five at the time, listened to our conversations, read many lawn signs, and felt the emotional tenor both in our home and in the homes of many of our friends. A few weeks before Election Day, she asked me, "Mama, if we lose, will you and Mommy have to get a divorce?"

Her fear was real and it paralleled the fear that many of us felt. Particularly in the context of the previous thirty ballot initiatives, in which the pro-LGBTQ movement had lost and state constitutions had been amended to narrowly define marriage, the context in which pro-LGBTQ religious mobilizing took place was one of steep odds. As a way to remind ourselves of the importance of doing the work whether or not we "won" in the short term, many of the religious organizers gathered once a month for a multifaith worship service entitled, "Healing Minnesota." Preaching at one of those services, I shared the following story as told by Rev. Dr. Howard Thurman, a mentor and teacher of Dr. Martin Luther King, Jr.:

> On one of our visits to Daytona Beach, I was eager to show my daughters some of my old haunts. We sauntered down the long street from the church to the riverfront. This had been the path of the procession to the baptismal ceremony in the Halifax River, which I had often described to them. We stopped here and there as I noted the changes that had

taken place since that far-off time. At length, we passed the playground of the white public schools. As soon as Olive and Anne saw the swings, they jumped for joy. "Look, Daddy, let's go over and swing!" This was the inescapable moment of truth that every black parent in America must face soon or late. What do you say to your child at the critical moment of primary encounter?

"You can't swing on those swings."

"Why?"

"When we get home and have some cold lemonade I will tell you." When we were home again, and had had our lemonade, Anne pressed for the answer. "We are home now, Daddy. Tell us."

I said, "It is against the law for us to use those swings, even though it is a public school. At present, only white children can play there. But it takes the state legislature, the courts, the sheriffs and the policemen, the white churches, the mayors, the banks and businesses, and the majority of the white people in the State of Florida—it takes all these to keep two little black girls from swinging in those swings. That is how important you are! Never forget, the estimate of your own importance and self-worth can be judged by how many weapons and how much power people are willing to use to control you and keep you in the place they have assigned to you. You are two very important little girls. Your presence can threaten the entire state of Florida."[1]

As I told my friends in that sermon, our experiences of justice and injustice are different. The struggle for LGBTQ justice is not the same as that for Civil Rights. Racism and homophobia, biphobia, and transphobia live and act in different ways. I did not want to pretend to co-opt Dr. Thurman's experience. But his wisdom gave us an important lesson. We live in a world whose laws and systems pressure us to teach our children that we and they are less than our neighbors.[2]

1. Howard Thurman, *With Head and Heart: The Autobiography of Howard Thurman* (Boston: Houghton Mifflin, 1981), 97.
2. Rebecca Voelkel, "Rooted in God's Love" (sermon, Healing Minnesota Service, Plymouth Congregational Church, Minneapolis, November 27, 2011). It is worth noting that marriage equality efforts are complicated. Marriage equality is an opportunity to "queer" marriage simply because queer bodies are inhabiting a marriage. In the face of hegemonic notions of dominance/ submission, ownership, and patriarchy, marriage equality offers opportunities to bust binaries and reenvision collaborative power, mutuality, and many of the values expressed in this book. However, many pro-LGBTQ activists have also noted that marriage equality came as a defensive response to ballot initiatives aimed at discriminating against LGBTQ families; it was not chosen

It was especially important for my LGBTQ allies in that amendment season, and it is no less important for us now, that we never forget just how important we are. Not that we are better than our neighbors, because we are not. But when we love each other, not because we must, but because we may; when we walk with each other over years, through good times and bad, not because we've made a contract recognized by the state, but because we have chosen to be friends, or lovers, or chosen family; when we stand together as a community—even in the face of lies and colonizing brutality—I believe we are beginning to grasp the truth that Paul writes about in his letter to the Romans:

> For I am convinced that neither death, nor life, nor angels, nor rulers, nor things present, nor things to come, nor powers, nor constitutional amendments nor height, nor depth, nor anything else in all creation, will be able to separate us from the love of God.[3]

In many ways, this book seeks to preach large the sermon I preached on that occasion. Its message: whether any single campaign or mobilization effort is "successful" is not the reason for any of our work and ministry for justice. We are called to be lovers in the name of God because it is faithful and just. There will be multiple setbacks because colonization and the forces of hegemonic oppression are real and persistently powerful. Even our policy "wins" do not mark the end. Even as the Civil Rights Act and the Voting Rights Act set policy against racism, our larger vision of a world of racial justice has not arrived;indeed we have witnessed their vulnerability in recent years. Even as the Violence Against Women Act continues to be renewed, gender justice has not been made manifest. Indeed, the past few years have seen a reemergence of self-satisfied Rape Culture with rapists (often white men) getting off with little or no time served. Even as the

---

as a proactive value or goal of the movement. Marriage can be the ultimate "domestication" of queerness or co-opting of that which is disruptive. It can establish a good queer / bad queer binary, with those who get married and participate in "normal" (i.e., heteronormative) family units being held up as models while those who advocate for chosen family, extended community, or other forms of family as being "bad queers."

3. Rom 8:38–39.

Supreme Court made same-sex marriage legal, our larger vision for the world has not come to pass. And with the elevation of virulent, self-professed homophobes in the highest offices of the land, this, too, may be vulnerable.

The forces of colonization and hegemonic oppression are strong. This is abundantly clear as we presently witness the resurgence of white supremacy in the election of Donald Trump and the violent suppression of peaceful, prayerful Water Protectors at Standing Rock. Indeed, the forces of colonization are alive and well. It is in this reality that our carnal relationship with an extravagantly loving God blesses us, embodies us with cellular creativity, and calls us into prophetic, resistant, and transformative ministries for the long haul.

My prayer is that this book will aid, support, and encourage us to engage this present moment. May it help foster our resistance, nurture our prophesying, and empower our revolutionary dreaming of the world God desires for all of us and, in dreaming it, begin to build it.

Glossary of Terms

This book brings together language and work from a variety of communities, movements, and traditions. This means that the words I use and the ways in which I use them may be familiar in some parts of the book but not in others. To make the book as accessible and clear as possible, I have shared below the ways in which I am using these terms. I hope it is helpful.

cisgender: Many people have a gender identity that matches what society says is appropriate for their biological sex and therefore are called cisgender. Cisgender means "matching gender." This term is used in relationship with transgender and gender non-conforming.[1]

colonization: The context and process by which one group of people employ power and resources to subjugate, oppress, marginalize, and/or kill another group or groups of people and exploit the land and its creatures. Colonization is marked by domination, hierarchies, violence, and the creation of scarcity through individual acts and through the creation of systems that enshrine and perpetuate colonizer/colonized relationships. In order to succeed, colonization requires accompanying cultural, philosophical, and theological hegemonies.

culturally competent: Acting in ways that recognize the cultural significance, differentiation, and humanity of a particular group of

---

1. Barbara Satin, *transACTION: A Transgender Curriculum for Churches and Religious Institutions* (Minneapolis: National Gay and Lesbian Task Force, 2007), 7.

people when relating to them or speaking about them. This includes paying attention to cultural particularities such as language, dress, relationship to time, and authority structures and roles, as well as acting in ways that honor them.

feminist theology: A theological tradition that seeks to employ a "hermeneutic of suspicion" in relationship to the Christian tradition. Feminist theology is suspicious toward a Christianity based solely on the testimony and story of men. It asks: "Where are the voices, experiences, and witness of women?" "What women might have been in this biblical story whose names are lost?" "What might we understand about theology, politics, or Jesus if we read the text and the tradition from the perspective of those marginalized and oppressed by misogyny and sexism?"[2]

gender identity: Unlike biological sex, which is assigned by others based on physical characteristics, gender identity refers to our internalized, deeply felt sense of being male, female, both, or neither. It can be different from the biological sex we were assigned at birth. Society is beginning to recognize that there are more than two categories of gender identity and is creating newly defined terms to reflect these normal variations of gender. Because gender identity is internal and personally defined, it is not visible to others—it is determined by the individual alone. Most of us have an early sense of our gender identity, and we may begin voicing this between the ages of two and four. This is not the only time a person's sense of gender identity deepens or solidifies; it may occur at other developmental stages, such as early adolescence or young adulthood. It may remain stable over time, or it may change. Sometimes, social pressures force an individual to stifle their gender identity until later in life—even though that person has experienced that identity since childhood.[3]

2. Early feminist theologians such as Mary Daly and Rosemary Radford Ruether emerged from the Roman Catholic tradition. For a powerful explanation of feminist theology, see Mary Daly, *Beyond God the Father: Toward a Philosophy of Women's Liberation* (Boston: Beacon Press, 1973), and Rosemary Radford Ruether, *Sexism and God-talk: Toward a Feminist Theology* (Boston: Beacon Press, 1983).
3. Satin, *transACTION*, 7.

gender non-conforming / gender variance: Gender variance refers to behaviors and interests that fit outside of what we consider "normal" for a person's assigned biological sex. We think of these people as having interests that are more typical of the "opposite" sex—for example, a girl who insists on having short hair and prefers to play football with the boys, or a boy who wears dresses and wishes to be a princess. These are considered gender-variant or gender non-conforming behaviors and interests. It is important to remember that "normal" behaviors or interests are culturally formed and may be different from one society to another.[4]

gender pronouns: One of the acts of inclusion and justice that many communities practice is to invite each person to identify the pronouns by which they ask to be referred. There are many options. These are but a few: he/him/his, she/her/hers, they/their/theirs, ze/hir, s/he. The importance of the exercise is to encourage the self-determination of each person and to begin to interrupt binaries.

genderqueer: People who identify as genderqueer may think of themselves as being both a man and a woman, as being neither a man nor a woman, or as falling completely outside the gender binary. Some wish to have certain features of the opposite sex but not all characteristics; others want to have all the characteristics and features. The terms "transgender" and "genderqueer" are not synonymous, but there is some overlap between people who identify as transgender and people who identify as genderqueer.[5]

hegemony: Hegemony describes at least two different foci: geopolitical and cultural. Geopolitical hegemony is indirect in which the *hegēmon* (leader state) rules geopolitically subordinate states by the implied means of power, the threat of force, rather than by direct military force. Cultural hegemony, a concept developed by Antonio Gramsci, refers to a context in which one social class can manipulate the system of values and mores of a society in order to create and establish a ruling class, by establishing a world view

4. Ibid.
5. Ibid., 10.

that justifies the status quo of domination of the poor and working classes by that ruling class. Liberation theologians have expanded cultural hegemony to include world views that justify domination based on race, sex, ability, age, sexual orientation, and gender identity.[6]

heteronormativity: Heteronormativity is the body of norms and hegemonies that hold that people fall into distinct and complementary genders (man and woman) with "natural" roles in life. It also holds that heterosexuality is the "normal" sexual orientation and states that sexual and marital relations are most (or only) fitting between a man and a woman. Consequently, a heteronormative view is the hegemonic imposition of a perceived alignment of biological sex, sexuality, gender identity, and gender roles.[7] For an examination of heteronormativity and its impact on queer people, see Adrienne Rich's "Compulsory Heterosexuality and Lesbian Existence."[8]

intersectionality: Intersectionality is a feminist sociological theory first highlighted by Kimberlé Crenshaw in 1989. Intersectionality is a methodology of studying the relationships among multiple dimensions and modalities of social relationships and subject formations. The theory suggests and seeks to examine how various biological, social, and cultural categories, such as gender, race, class, ability, and other axes of identity interact on multiple and often simultaneous levels, contributing to systematic social inequality. Intersectionality holds that the classical conceptualizations of oppression within society, such as racism, sexism, homophobia, and religion-based bigotry, do not act independently of one another; instead, these forms of oppression interrelate, creating a system

6. Antonio Gramsci, *Prison Notebooks*, vol. 1, ed. Joseph A. Buttigieg, trans. Joseph A. Buttigieg and Antonio Callari (New York: Columbia University Press, 1992), 233–38.
7. Karen Lovaas and Mercilee M. Jenkins, "Charting a Path through the 'Desert of Nothing,'" in *Sexualities and Communication in Everyday Life: A Reader* (Thousand Oaks, CA: Sage Publications, 2007), 98.
8. Adrienne Rich, "Compulsory Heterosexuality and Lesbian Existence," *Signs* 5, no. 4 (Summer 1980): 631–60.

of oppression that reflects the "intersections" of multiple forms of discrimination.

intersex: Intersex is a general term used for a variety of conditions in which a person is born with a reproductive or sexual anatomy that doesn't seem to fit the typical definitions of female or male.[9]

justice: Justice comes from the biblical understanding of *mishpat* and has to do with treating people equitably. It refers to both the response to an individual's wrongdoing as well as the construction of right relationships, caring communities, and systems of protection. The Bible most often names the construction of just relationships, communities, and systems in reference to protecting those who do not hold power in any given system, namely the widow, the orphan, the immigrant, and the poor.

lesbian: Lesbian is the term used to describe those individuals whose biological sex is female and/or whose gender identity is woman whose primary emotional, affectional, and sexual desires are with and for other individuals whose biological sex is female and/or whose gender identity is woman. Lesbian is also used to describe the community and culture that is created by those who identify as lesbian.

liberation theology: A theological tradition that understands God's "preferential option for the poor and marginalized" and that recognizes that some of the most insidious and powerful manifestations of sin are in systems of economic and social oppression.[10]

mujerista: A mujerista is someone who makes a preferential option for Latina women's struggle for liberation. Mujeristas struggle to liberate themselves not as individuals but as members of a Latinx community.[11]

---

9. Intersex Society of North America, "What Is Intersex?," accessed May 24, 2016, http://tinyurl.com/jhhuazc.
10. One of the earliest theologians who articulated a theology of liberation was Gustavo Gutiérrez, a Peruvian theologian and priest whose 1971 *A Theology of Liberation: History, Politics, Salvation* was one of the first to articulate a preferential option for the poor. See Gustavo Gutiérrez, *A Theology of Liberation: History, Politics, and Salvation* (Maryknoll, NY: Orbis Books, 1973).
11. Because Spanish is a gendered language, activists use an "x" at the end of a word to connote a multiplicity of endings in order to connote a multiplicity of possible genders.

queer theology: A theological tradition that seeks to take the lives and experiences of lesbian, gay, bisexual, transgender, queer, and intersex (LGBTQI) people seriously. By examining Christianity through the lens of LGBTQI experience, queer theology seeks to break many categories that were once assumed static: gender binaries of male and female, sexual categories, categorical "wrong" and categorical "right." Queer theology claims embodiment as a site of revelation and gender and sexuality as sacred ways to understand God's movement in the world. Queer theology often sets about creating hybrids, putting together things that once were considered opposites or unrelated such as queer Christian; sex as a site of revelation; and African American, HIV-positive poet, and religious activist.[12]

sexuality: There are multiple definitions of sexuality, but one that I have found most helpful comes from *Sexuality and the Sacred*, edited by Sandra Longfellow and James B. Nelson. In their introduction, they suggest "sexuality is the Divine invitation to find our destinies, not in loneliness, but in deep connection."[13] Some have criticized this definition as not being embodied enough; others suggest it could also define spirituality, which is a similar gift from God that brings connection, communion, and deeper understanding of God and of the human community.

sexual orientation: Sexual orientation describes an enduring pattern of attraction that is romantic and/or sexual to persons of the opposite sex, to persons of the same sex, or to both sexes, as well as the gender identities that accompany them. These attractions are generally subsumed under heterosexuality, homosexuality, and bisexuality, while asexuality (the lack of romantic or sexual attraction to others) is sometimes identified as a fourth category.

spirituality: Spirituality is the orientation, desire, and practice of

---

12. As in liberation and feminist theologies, there are many queer theologians, but one who has sought to articulate what queer theology means is Robert Goss. His *Queering Christ: Beyond Jesus Acted Up* seeks to lay out some of the hallmarks of queer theology. See Robert Goss, *Queering Christ: Beyond Jesus Acted Up* (Cleveland, OH: Pilgrim Press, 2002).
13. James B. Nelson and Sandra P. Longfellow, eds., *Sexuality and the Sacred: Sources for Theological Reflection* (Louisville: Westminster John Knox, 1994), xiv.

connecting with the Divine for the purposes of illumination, relationship, and intimacy. Spirituality refers to individual as well as communal contexts.

third space: A term used by African American and First Nation activists to describe the time and location in which collective dreaming (substantially unencumbered by the conditions of oppression and colonization) happens. Third space is in relationship with first space—which is the condition of colonization, injustice, and oppression—and second space—which is the analysis and deconstruction of the forces that create first space.

transgender: Those persons who have a gender identity that differs from their assigned biological sex are called transgender. Transgender is an umbrella term that includes transsexuals, cross-dressers, and intersex people, and just about anybody else who doesn't conform to the traditional model of sex/gender. Transgender is the most general, inclusive term but does not fully address the wide variety of non-conforming gender expressions that exist.[14]

two-spirit: Two-spirit is a name used within Indian, Native American, Indigenous, and First Nation communities to refer to those who are gender variant and/or perform multiple genders. Two-spirit is an English translation of an Ojibwe word and is used by indigenous organizers for intertribal LGBTQ two-spirit organizing. "The Two Spirit term was adopted in 1990 at an Indigenous lesbian and gay international gathering to encourage the replacement of the term berdache, which means, 'passive partner in sodomy, boy prostitute.' A Two Spirit person is a male-bodied or female-bodied person with a masculine or feminine essence. Two Spirits can cross social gender roles, gender expression, and sexual orientation."[15]

womanism: "'Womanist is to feminist as purple is to lavender'—Alice Walker. Womanism is a feminist term coined by Alice Walker. It is a reaction to the realization that 'feminism' does not encompass

14. Satin, transACTION, 7.
15. Two-Spirit Resource Center, "Two-Spirit 101," NativeOUT, accessed May 24, 2016, http://tinyurl.com/hevnd4l.

the perspectives of Black women. It is a feminism that is 'stronger in color,' nearly identical to 'Black Feminism.' However, Womanism does not need to be prefaced by the word 'Black,' the word automatically concerns black women."[16]

---

16. Emma Gunde, *A Feminist Theory Dictionary* (blog), Gender and Critical Inquiry course, Portland State University, July 17, 2007, http://tinyurl.com/hkweuqg.

Bibliography

Agosín, Marjorie. *I Lived on Butterfly Hill*. Translated by E. M. O'Connor. New York: Atheneum, 2014.

Alston, Macky. "The Power and Pleasure You Can Unleash When Your Inner Artist Joins Your Inner Activist." *The Huffington Post*, February 17, 2015. http://tinyurl.com/zrv32fr.

Althaus-Reid, Marcella. *Indecent Theology: Theological Perversions in Sex, Gender and Politics*. New York: Routledge, 2000.

Anzaldúa, Gloria. Borderlands/La Frontera: The New Mestiza. 4th ed. San Francisco: Aunt Lute Books, 2012.

Anzaldúa, Gloria, and AnaLouise Keating. *This Bridge We Call Home: Radical Visions for Transformation*. New York: Routledge, 2002.

Baldwin, James. "The Black Scholar Interviews James Baldwin." In *Conversations with James Baldwin*, edited by Fred L. Standley and Louis H. Pratt, 142–58. Jackson: University Press of Mississippi, 1989.

_____. "On Being White and Other Lies." *Essence*, April 1984.

Beauvoir, Simone de. *The Second Sex*. Translated and edited by H. M. Parshley. New York: Vintage Books, 1989.

Boring, Wendy, John A. Geter, and Stefano Penna. "A Maternal Body and a Body with AIDS: Theological Reflections on Carnal Knowledge and the Incarnate God." Paper presented at the annual meeting of the American Academy of Religion, San Francisco, November 24, 1997.

Braaten, Carl E. "The Person of Jesus Christ." In *Christian Dogmatics, Vol. 1*, edited by Carl E. Braaten and Robert W. Jenson, 465–569. Philadelphia: Fortress Press, 1984.

Brezina, Corona. *Sojourner Truth's "Ain't I a Woman?" Speech: A Primary Source Investigation.* New York: Rosen Central Primary Source, 2005.

Bright, Susie. *Susie Sexpert's Lesbian Sex World.* Santa Cruz, CA: Bright Stuff, 2008.

Brock, Rita Nakashima. *Journeys by Heart: A Christology of Erotic Power.* New York: Crossroad, 1988.

Brunner, Emil. *The Christian Doctrine of God.* Translated by Olive Wyon. Philadelphia: Westminster, 1950.

Caruso, Barbara. "On Being Redundant: Freedom Is Not Once." Baccalaureate address, Earlham College, Richmond, IN, June 9, 1991.

Catholics 4 Marriage Equality. "For All the Children . . . Vote 'No' in November in Minnesota." YouTube video, 6:25, posted August 16, 2012. http://tinyurl.com/gqxqwe9.

Cheng, Patrick S. *Radical Love: An Introduction to Queer Theology.* New York: Seabury Books, 2011.

_____. *Rainbow Theology: Bridging Race, Sexuality, and Spirit.* New York: Seabury Books, 2013.

Cohen, Steven M., Caryn Aviv, and Ari Y. Kelman. "Gay, Jewish, or Both? Sexual Orientation and Jewish Involvement." *Journal of Jewish Communal Service* 84, no. 1/2 (Winter/Spring 2009): 154–66.

Copleston, Frederick. *A History of Philosophy.* 9 vols. New York: Doubleday, 1985.

Crenshaw, Kimberlé W. "Mapping the Margins: Intersectionality, Identity Politics, and Violence Against Women of Color." *Stanford Law Review* 43, no. 6 (1991): 1241–99.

Crossan, John Dominic. *The Essential Jesus: Original Sayings and Earliest Images.* San Francisco: HarperSanFrancisco, 1998.

Daly, Mary. *Beyond God the Father: Toward a Philosophy of Women's Liberation.* Boston: Beacon Press, 1973.

Douglas, Kelly Brown. *Sexuality and the Black Church: A Womanist Perspective.* Maryknoll, NY: Orbis Books, 1999.

Dreher, Rod. "'Paradise Road' Camp Prisoners Recall the Music of Survival." *Lubbock Avalanche-Journal,* April 24, 1997.

Duncombe, Stephen. *Dream: Re-Imagining Progressive Politics in an Age of Fantasy.* New York: New Press, 2007.

Esquivel, Julia. *Threatened with Resurrection: Prayers and Poems from an Exiled Guatemalan*. Elgin, IL: Brethren Press, 1994.

Farley, Margaret. *Just Love: A Framework for Christian Sexual Ethics*. New York: Continuum International, 2006.

Fernandez, Eleazar S. *Reimagining the Human: Theological Anthropology in Response to Systemic Evil*. St. Louis: Chalice Press, 2004.

Font, Pedro. *Font's Complete Diary of the Second Anza Expedition*. Translated and edited by Hubert Eugène Bolton. Vol. 4 of *Anza's California Expeditions*. Berkeley: University of California Press, 1930.

Fox, George. *The Works of George Fox*. Edited by T. H. S. Wallace. State College, PA: New Foundation Publication, George Fox Fund, 1990.

Fox, Matthew. "Moving Beyond a Cross Fetish: The Empty Tomb and Creation Spirituality." *Tikkun*, October 28, 2012. http://tinyurl.com/jfmlcx2.

_____. *Original Blessing: A Primer in Creation Spirituality*. New York: Penguin Putnam, 2000.

Goldberg, Michelle. "National Organization for Marriage Memos Reveal Racial Wedge Strategy." *The Daily Beast*, March 27, 2012. http://tinyurl.com/jjk8nnb.

Goldman, Emma. *Living My Life*. New York: Dover Publications, 1970.

Goss, Robert. *Queering Christ: Beyond Jesus Acted Up*. Cleveland, OH: Pilgrim Press, 2002.

Gramsci, Antonio. *Prison Notebooks*. Vol. 1. Edited by Joseph A. Buttigieg. Translated by Joseph A. Buttigieg and Antonio Callari. New York: Columbia University Press, 1992.

Grant, Jacquelyn. *White Women's Christ and Black Women's Jesus: Feminist Christology and Womanist Response*. Atlanta: Scholars Press, 1989.

Grassroots Policy Project. *The 3 Faces of Power*. February 2007. PDF. http://tinyurl.com/hh5dma7.

Gunde, Emma. "Womanism." *A Feminist Theory Dictionary* (blog). Gender and Critical Inquiry course, Portland State University, July 17, 2007. http://tinyurl.com/hkweuqg.

Gutiérrez, Gustavo. *A Theology of Liberation: History, Politics, and Salvation*. Maryknoll, NY: Orbis Books, 1973.

Harness, Ashley. "Spiritual Care for Justice and Wholeness: A Case Study for

LGBTQ Movement Building." Master's thesis, Union Theological Seminary, 2012.

Harvey, Jennifer. *Dear White Christians: For Those Still Longing for Racial Reconciliation*. Grand Rapids: Eerdmans, 2014.

Hayes, Michael A., and David Tombs. *Truth and Memory: The Church and Human Rights in El Salvador and Guatemala*. Leominster, UK: Gracewing Publishing, 2001.

Hellwig, Monika K. "Eschatology." In *Systematic Theology: Roman Catholic Perspectives*, edited by Francis Schüssler Fiorenza and John P. Galvin, 2:347–72. Minneapolis: Fortress Press, 1991.

Heyward, Carter. "Sexuality, Love and Justice." In *Weaving the Visions: New Patterns in Feminist Spirituality*, edited by Judith Plaskow and Carol P. Christ, 293–301. New York: Harper & Row, 1989.

Hill Collins, Patricia. *Black Feminist Thought: Knowledge, Consciousness, and the Politics of Empowerment*. New York: Routledge, 1991.

Hollibaugh, Amber L. *My Dangerous Desires: A Queer Girl Dreaming Her Way Home*. Durham, NC: Duke University Press, 2000.

hooks, bell. *Black Looks: Race and Representation*. Boston: South End Press, 1992.

Hunt, Mary E. "Bodies Don't Lie: A Feminist Theological Perspective on Embodiment." Lecture given at the World Forum on Theology and Liberation, Belém, Brazil, January 24, 2009.

_____. *Fierce Tenderness: A Feminist Theology of Friendship*. New York: Crossroad, 1991.

_____. "Lovingly Lesbian: Toward a Feminist Theology of Friendship." In *Sexuality and the Sacred: Sources for Theological Reflection*, edited by Marvin M. Ellison and Kelly Brown Douglas, 169–82. 2nd ed. Louisville: Westminster John Knox, 2010.

Intersex Society of North America. "What Is Intersex?" Accessed May 24, 2016. http://tinyurl.com/jhhuazc.

Johnson, James Weldon. "The Creation." In *The Book of American Negro Poetry*, 117–22. New York: Harcourt, Brace, 1922.

Johnson, Jay Emerson. *Peculiar Faith: Queer Theology for Christian Witness*. New York: Seabury Books, 2014.

Joiner, Lottie L. "Remembering Civil Rights Heroine Fannie Lou Hamer: 'I'm

Sick and Tired of Being Sick and Tired.'" *The Daily Beast*, September 2, 2014. http://tinyurl.com/hbv342n.

Jordan, Winthrop D. *The White Man's Burden: Historical Origins of Racism in the United States.* London: Oxford University Press, 1974.

Jung, Patricia Beattie, Mary E. Hunt, and Radhika Balakrishnan. *Good Sex: Feminist Perspectives from the World's Religions.* New Brunswick, NJ: Rutgers University Press, 2001.

Katz, Jonathan Ned. *Gay American History.* New York: Plume, 1992.

Kinsey, Alfred C. *Sexual Behavior in the Human Female.* Philadelphia: Saunders, 1953.

LaCugna, Catherine Mowry. "The Trinitarian Mystery of God." In *Systematic Theology: Roman Catholic Perspectives*, edited by Francis Schüssler Fiorenza and John P. Galvin, 1:149–92. Minneapolis: Fortress Press, 1991.

L'Engle, Madeleine. *A Wind in the Door.* New York: Farrar, Straus & Giroux, 1973.

LGBT Religious Archives Network and GLBT Historical Society. "Clergy and Homosexual Persons Converge in San Francisco: Dialogue." The Council on Religion and the Homosexual exhibit. LGBT Religious Archives Network, accessed May 19, 2015. http://tinyurl.com/z27gzp5.

Lioi, Anthony. "The Best-Loved Bones: Spirit and History in Anzaldúa's 'Entering into the Serpent.'" *Feminist Studies* 34, no. 1/2, Chicana Studies Issue (Spring/Summer 2008): 73–98.

Lorde, Audre. "Uses of the Erotic: The Erotic as Power." In *Sexuality and the Sacred: Sources for Theological Reflection*, edited by Marvin M. Ellison and Kelly Brown Douglas, 75–79. 2nd ed. Louisville: Westminster John Knox, 2010.

Loulan, JoAnn. *The Lesbian Erotic Dance: Butch, Femme, Androgyny, and Other Rhythms.* San Francisco: Spinsters, 1990.

_____. *Lesbian Passion: Loving Ourselves and Each Other.* San Francisco: Aunt Lute Books, 1987.

_____. *Lesbian Sex.* San Francisco: Spinsters, 1984.

Lovaas, Karen, and Mercilee M. Jenkins. "Charting a Path through the 'Desert of Nothing.'" In *Sexualities and Communication in Everyday Life: A Reader*, 98–106. Thousand Oaks, CA: Sage Publications, 2007.

Malcolm X. *The Autobiography of Malcolm X.* New York: Ballantine Books, 1973.

Mogul, Joey L., Andrea J. Ritchie, and Kay Whitlock, eds. *Queer (In)justice: The Criminalization of LGBT People in the United States.* Boston: Beacon Press, 2011.

Morrison, Toni. *Beloved.* New York: Penguin, 1987.

Morton, Nelle. *The Journey Is Home.* Boston: Beacon Press, 1985.

Movement Advancement Project and Center for American Progress. *Unjust: How the Broken Criminal Justice System Fails Transgender People.* May 2016. PDF. http://tinyurl.com/gvcx5n4.

Myers, Ched. *Binding the Strong Man: A Political Reading of Mark's Story of Jesus.* Maryknoll, NY: Orbis Books, 1994.

Nelson, James B. *Body Theology.* Louisville: Westminster John Knox, 1992.

Nelson, James B., and Sandra P. Longfellow, eds. *Sexuality and the Sacred: Sources for Theological Reflection.* Louisville: Westminster John Knox, 1994.

Niemöller, Martin. *Martin Niemöller: 1892-1984.* Edited by James Bentley. New York: Free Press, 1984.

_____. *Of Guilt and Hope.* Translated by Renee Spodheim. New York: Philosophical Library, 1947.

Orwell, George. *1984.* New York: Signet Classics, 1949.

Park, Sung, Lisa Weiner-Mahfuz, and Rebecca Voelkel. "Practice Spirit, Do Justice Opening Plenary." Lecture given at "Practice Spirit, Do Justice: Creating Change Conference," Minneapolis, February 3, 2011.

Pellauer, Mary D. "The Moral Significance of Female Orgasm: Toward Sexual Ethics That Celebrates Women's Sexuality." *Journal of Feminist Studies in Religion* 9, no. 1/2 (Spring/Fall 1993): 161–82.

Pérez, Laura E. "Decolonizing Sexuality and Spirituality in Chicana Feminist and Queer Art." *Tikkun,* July/August 2010. http://tinyurl.com/zl5jrje.

Plaskow, Judith. *Standing Again at Sinai: Judaism from a Feminist Perspective.* San Francisco: Harper & Row, 1990.

Reagon, Bernice Johnson. "Convocation Address." Lecture given at Earlham College, Richmond, IN, April 19, 1990.

Rich, Adrienne. "Compulsory Heterosexuality and Lesbian Existence." *Signs* 5, no. 4 (Summer 1980): 631–60.

Ruether, Rosemary Radford. *Sexism and God-talk: Toward a Feminist Theology.* Boston: Beacon Press, 1983.

Satin, Barbara. *transACTION: A Transgender Curriculum for Churches and Religious Institutions*. Minneapolis: National Gay and Lesbian Task Force, 2007.

Schleiermacher, Friedrich. "Addresses on Religion (1799)." In *A History of Christianity: Readings in the History of the Church*, edited by Ray C. Petry and Clyde L. Manschreck, 335–41. Grand Rapids: Baker, 1981.

Schneider, Laurel. "Promiscuous Incarnation." In *The Embrace of Eros: Bodies, Desires, and Sexuality in Christianity*, edited by Margaret D. Kamitsuka, 231–44. Minneapolis: Fortress Press, 2010.

_____. "What Race Is Your Sex?" In *Disrupting White Supremacy from Within: White People on What We Need to Do*, edited by Jennifer Harvey, Karin A. Case, and Robin Hawley Gorsline, 142–62. Cleveland, OH: Pilgrim Press, 2004.

Segrest, Mab. *Born to Belonging: Writings on Spirit and Justice*. New Brunswick, NJ: Rutgers University Press, 2002.

Smith, Andrea. *Conquest: Sexual Violence and the American Indian Genocide*. Cambridge, MA: South End, 2005.

Spirit of the Lakes United Church of Christ. "A Service of Communion." In *A Place in God's Heart, A Place at Christ's Table: Worship Resources for the Welcoming Church Movement*, edited by David Lohman, 44–45. Minneapolis: Institute for Welcoming Resources of the National Gay and Lesbian Task Force, 2007.

Sponheim, Paul R. "Sin and Evil." In *Christian Dogmatics, Vol. 1*, edited by Carl E. Braaten and Robert W. Jenson, 363–64. Philadelphia: Fortress Press, 1984.

Thurman, Howard. *With Head and Heart: The Autobiography of Howard Thurman*. Boston: Houghton Mifflin, 1981.

Turney, Kelly, ed. *Shaping Sanctuary: Proclaiming God's Grace in an Inclusive Church*. Chicago: Reconciling Congregation Program, 2000.

Two-Spirit Resource Center. "Two-Spirit 101." NativeOUT, accessed May 24, 2016. http://tinyurl.com/hevnd4l.

Voelkel, Rebecca. "Highlander Singers, Jesus Challengers and Outrageous Street Dancers." Sermon given at Bishops and Elders Council Meeting, Dallas, TX, September 10, 2006.

_____. "LGBT Activism as Ministry." Lecture given as part of the Earle Lectures, Center for Lesbian and Gay Studies in Religion and Ministry at Pacific School of Religion, Berkeley, CA, January 27, 2009.

_____. "Rooted in God's Love." Sermon given at the Healing Minnesota Service, Plymouth Congregational Church, Minneapolis, November 27, 2011.

_____. "This Complex, Complicated Calling." Sermon given at Lyndale United Church of Christ, Minneapolis, August 3, 2014.

_____. "Timeless Time." Sermon given at Lyndale United Church of Christ, Minneapolis, July 12, 2013.

_____. *A Time to Build Up: Analysis of the No on Proposition 8 Campaign and Its Implications for Future Pro-LGBTQQIA Religious Organizing.* Minneapolis: National Gay and Lesbian Task Force, 2009.

_____. "Women, Our Bodies and Spirit." DMin project, United Theological Seminary of the Twin Cities, 2012.

Voelkel, Rebecca, Vicki Wunsch, David Lohman, and Tim Feiertag. *Building an Inclusive Church: A Welcoming Toolkit.* Minneapolis: National Gay and Lesbian Task Force, 2013.

Voelkel-Haugen, Rebecca, and Marie M. Fortune. *Sexual Abuse Prevention: A Course of Study for Teenagers, Revised and Updated.* Cleveland, OH: United Church Press, 1996.

Walker, Alice. *The Color Purple.* Orlando, FL: Harcourt, 2003.

_____. *Possessing the Secret of Joy.* New York: Harcourt, Brace, Jovanovich, 1992.

Watson, Veronica T. *The Souls of White Folks: African American Writers Theorize Whiteness.* Jackson: University Press of Mississippi, 2013.

Wesley, John. *John Wesley.* Edited by Albert C. Outler. New York: Oxford University Press, 1964.

West, Cornel. "A Love Supreme." *The Occupied Wall Street Journal,* November 18, 2011. http://tinyurl.com/hn7srrq.

Wiesel, Elie. *Night.* New York: Bantam Books, 1982.

Williams, Delores. "Re-Imagining Jesus." Lecture given at "Re-Imagining: A Global Theological Conference by Women: For Men and Women," Minneapolis, November 5, 1993.

Zemsky, Beth. "Netroots Pre-Conference Intersectional Meeting of Multifaith Leaders." Presentation at the Netroots Conference, Providence, RI, June 6, 2012.

Zemsky, Beth, and David Mann. "Building Organizations in a Movement Moment." *Social Policy* 38, no. 3 (Spring/Summer 2008): 9–17.

Index